The Castle Lectures in Ethics,
Politics, and Economics

ON
TOLERATION

MICHAEL WALZER

Yale University Press   New Haven and London

Designed by James J. Johnson and set in Schneidler Roman type by Tseng Information Systems, Inc., Durham, North Carolina. Printed in the United States of America by Vail-Ballou Press, Binghamton, New York.

Library of Congress Cataloging-in-Publication Data

Walzer, Michael.
On toleration / Michael Walzer.
p.   cm. — (The Castle lectures in ethics, politics, and economics)
    Includes bibliographical references and index.
    ISBN 0-300-07019-5 (cloth : alk. paper)

    1. Human rights.   2. Toleration.   3. Pluralism (Social sciences).
4. Multiculturalism.   I. Title.   II. Series.
JC574.W147   1997
305.8—dc21   96-47779

A catalogue record for this book is available from the British Library.

The paper in this book meets the guidelines for permanence and durability of the Committee on Production Guidelines for Book Longevity of the Council on Library Resources.

10 9 8 7 6 5 4 3 2 1

Parts of this book were given
as the Castle Lectures
in Yale's Program in Ethics, Politics, and Economics,
delivered by Michael Walzer at Yale University in 1996.

The Castle Lectures were endowed by
Mr. John K. Castle. They honor his ancestor the
Reverend James Pierpont, one of Yale's original founders.
Given by established public figures, Castle Lectures
are intended to promote reflection on the moral
foundations of society and government and
to enhance understanding of ethical
issues facing individuals in our
complex modern
society.

For the next generation

SARAH and JOHN

REBECCA and KEITH

and the next

JOSEPH

and

KATYA

Contents

Preface

As an American Jew, I grew up thinking of myself as an object of toleration. It was only much later that I recognized myself as a subject too, an agent called upon to tolerate others, including fellow Jews whose idea of what Jewishness meant differed radically from my own. My dawning sense of the United States as a country where everyone had to tolerate everyone else (a formula I shall explain later on) was the starting point of this essay. It led me to reflect on the ways in which other countries were different, and only sometimes intolerably different. All the world is not America!

Tolerating and being tolerated is a little like Aristotle's ruling and being ruled: it is the work of democratic citizens. I don't think that it is easy or insignificant work. Toleration itself is often underestimated, as if it is the least we can do for our fellows, the most minimal of their entitlements. In fact, tolerance (the attitude) takes many different forms, and toleration (the practice) can be arranged in different ways. Even the most grudging forms and precarious arrangements are very good things, sufficiently rare in human history that they require not only practical but also theoretical appreciation. As with other things that we value, we have to ask what it is that sustains toleration, how it works: that is the chief aim of this essay. Here I want only to suggest what it is that toleration sustains. It sustains life itself, because persecution is often to the death, and it also sustains common lives, the different communities in which we live. Toleration makes difference possible; difference makes toleration necessary.

A defense of toleration doesn't have to be a defense of difference. It can be, and often is, nothing more than an argument from necessity. But I write here with a high regard for difference, though not for every instance of it. In social, political, and cultural life, I prefer the many to the one. At the same time, I recognize that each regime of toleration must be singular and unified to some degree, capable of engaging the loyalty of its members. Coexistence requires a politically stable and morally legitimate arrangement, and this too is an object of value. Conceivably, there is a single best arrangement among all the possible ones, but I am inclined to doubt this proposition; I shall argue against it in the introduction. In any case, I shall attempt no more than a description of some of the possibilities and then an analysis and defense of the one that seems best for us here and now, Americans about to enter the twenty-first century—the one that best fits, and strengthens and enhances, our actual manyness.

On Toleration

How to Write About Toleration

Philosophical argument in recent years has often taken a proceduralist form: the philosopher imagines an original position, an ideal speech situation, or a conversation in a spaceship. Each of these is constituted by a set of constraints, rules of engagement, as it were, for the participating parties. The parties represent the rest of us. They reason, bargain, or talk within the constraints, which are designed to impose the formal criteria of any morality: absolute impartiality or some functional equivalent thereof. Assuming that the imposition is successful, the conclusions the parties reach can plausibly be regarded as morally authoritative. We are thus provided with governing principles for all our actual reasoning, bargaining, and talking—indeed, for all our political, social, and economic activity—in real world conditions. We ought to make these principles effective, so far as we are able, in our own lives and our own societies.[1]

In the pages that follow, I have adopted a different approach, which I mean to explain and defend in this brief introduction. I shall not attempt a systematic philosophical argument, though in the essay as a whole all the necessary features of such an argument will at least make an appearance: readers will find some general methodological indications and reasons here, and then an extended illustration with historical examples, an analysis of practical problems, and a tentative and incomplete conclusion, which is all that the approach allows. My subject is toleration—or, perhaps better, the peaceful coexistence of groups of people with different histories, cultures, and identities, which is what toleration makes possible. I begin with the proposition that peaceful coexistence (of a certain sort: I am not writing here about the coexistence of masters and slaves) is always a good thing. Not because people always in fact value it— they often obviously don't. The sign of its goodness is that they are so strongly inclined to say that they value it: they can't justify themselves, to themselves or to one another, without endorsing the value of peaceful coexistence and of the life and liberty that it serves.[2] This is a fact about the moral world—at least in the limited sense that the burden of argument falls on those who would reject these values. It is the practitioners of religious persecution, forced assimilation, crusading warfare, or "ethnic cleansing" who need to justify themselves, and they mostly do that not by defending what they are doing but by denying that they are doing it.

Peaceful coexistence, however, can take very different political forms, with different implications for everyday moral life—that is, for the actual interactions and mutual involvements of individual men and women. No one of these forms is universally valid. Beyond the minimalist claim for the value of peace, and the rules of forbearance that it entails (which match, roughly, the standard account of basic human rights), there are no principles that govern all the regimes of toleration or that require us to act in all circum-

stances, in all times and places, on behalf of a particular
set of political or constitutional arrangements. Proceduralist arguments won't help us here precisely because they are
not differentiated by time and place; they are not properly
circumstantial. The alternative that I mean to defend is a
historical and contextual account of toleration and coexistence, one that examines the different forms that these have
actually taken and the norms of everyday life appropriate
to each. It is necessary to look both at the ideal versions of
these practical arrangements and at their characteristic, historically documented distortions. We must consider as well
how the arrangements are experienced by different participants—both groups and individuals, both those who benefit
and those who are harmed—and then how they are seen by
outsiders, participants in the other regimes of toleration.

But isn't this a merely positivist or, worse, a relativist analysis? So long as there is no superior standpoint or
authoritative participant, how can we possibly arrive at a
critical standard? How can we rank and order the different regimes? I don't propose to do that, and I don't feel
any anxiety about not doing it. It doesn't seem plausible
to me that the sorts of political arrangements that I want
to consider—multinational empires and nation-states, say,
or the historical examples of each of these (Ptolomaic or
Roman Alexandria, the Ottoman empire, Hapsburg Austro-
Hungary, contemporary Italy, France, Norway, and so on)—
can be ranked in a single series, as if we could assign to each
some quantity of moral value: seven, nineteen, or thirty-one
and a half.

No doubt we can say that an arrangement likely to collapse into persecution and civil war is worse than one that
is more stable. But we can't say that an arrangement that
favors, for example, the survival of groups over the freedom

of individuals is systematically inferior to one that favors freedom over group survival—for groups are made up of individuals, many of whom, it is clear, would freely choose the first sort of arrangement over the second. Nor can we say that state neutrality and voluntary association, on the model of John Locke's "Letter on Toleration," is the only or best way of dealing with religious and ethnic pluralism. It is a very good way, one that is adapted to the experience of Protestant congregations in certain sorts of societies, but its reach beyond that experience and those societies has to be argued, not simply assumed. Radical attacks on individual freedom and associational rights can readily be condemned, and so can military or political (but not intellectual) challenges to the survival of a particular group: these are inconsistent with minimal coexistence. Beyond that, comparisons across arrangements are morally and politically helpful in thinking about where we are and what alternatives might be available to us, but they do not yield authoritative judgments.

The value of a close and circumstantial account of the different regimes of toleration, in both their ideal and actual versions, lies in just that helpfulness. For although the regimes are political or cultural wholes, with their advantages and disadvantages closely connected, they are not organic wholes. It is not the case that if some of their internal connections were broken or rearranged the regime would be condemned to political death. Every reform is not a transformation, and even transformations can be accomplished incrementally, over long periods of time. Conflict and trouble are sure to be features of any such process, but radical disruption and breakdown are not. If this or that aspect of an arrangement *there* seems likely to be useful *here,* with suitable modifications, we can work for a reform of that sort, aiming at what is best for us given the groups we value and the individuals we are.

What is not possible, however, is to take all the "nicest" features of each of the different arrangements and combine them—under the assumption that because of their similar niceness (the appeal they have in our eyes), they will in fact fit together and make an effective and harmonious unity. Sometimes, at least, and probably very often, the things we admire in a particular historical arrangement are functionally related to the things we fear or dislike.[3] It is an example of what might be called "bad utopianism" to imagine that we can reproduce or imitate the first and avoid the second. Philosophy has to be historically informed and sociologically competent if it is to avoid bad utopianism and acknowledge the hard choices that must often be made in political life. The harder the choices are, the less likely it is that one outcome, and one only, warrants philosophical approval. Perhaps we should choose this way here and that way there, this way now, that way at some future time. Perhaps all our choices should be tentative and experimental, always subject to revision or even reversal.

The idea that our choices are not determined by a single universal principle (or an interconnected set of principles) and that the right choice here might not be similarly right there is, strictly speaking, a relativist idea. The best political arrangement is relative to the history and culture of the people whose lives it will arrange. This seems to me an obvious point. But I am not advocating an unconstrained relativism, for no arrangement, and no feature of an arrangement, is a moral option unless it provides for some version of peaceful coexistence (and thereby upholds basic human rights). We choose within limits, and I suspect that the real disagreement among philosophers is not whether such limits exist—no one seriously believes that they don't—but how wide they are. The best way to estimate that width is to describe a range of options and to make the case for the plausibility and limitations of each within its historical context. I won't have much to say about the arrangements that get ruled out entirely—the monolithic religious or totalitarian political regimes. It is enough to name them and to remind readers of their historical reality. Set against that reality, peaceful coexistence is clearly an important and substantive moral principle.

To argue that different groups and/or individuals should be allowed to coexist in peace is not to argue that every actual or imaginable difference should be tolerated. The different arrangements that I am going to describe are in fact differentially tolerant of practices that the majority of their participants find strange or abhorrent—and then, obviously, differentially tolerant of the men and women who practice them. We can, therefore, classify the different arrangements, the different regimes of toleration, as more or less tolerant, and even establish (with many historical qualifications) a rank ordering from less to more. But when we look closely at some of the practices in question, it will quickly become apparent that this is not a moral ranking. The toleration of problematic practices varies across the different regimes in a complex way, and the judgments we make of the variance are likely to be similarly complex.

I mean to represent this complexity in my accounts of the different regimes and of the problems they all confront—and then, again, in the speculations about contemporary America with which this essay ends. The forms of coexistence have never been more widely debated than they are today, because the immediacy of difference, the everyday encounter with otherness, has never been so widely experienced. Watching television or reading the daily papers, it might seem that this experience is increasingly similar around the world. We are tempted, perhaps, to formulate a single response. But even highly similar encounters and transactions are necessarily differentiated when they engage different groups of people and when they are reflected on by men and women with different histories and expectations. Experience is always, necessarily, culturally mediated, and I have aimed to respect the difference that mediation makes. Hence I suggest my own view of how things should go, how peaceful coexistence might best be arranged, only with reference to my own time and place, my own American reality. At the end of this essay, I join, tentatively and experimentally, the debate about "multiculturalism."[4] But I don't believe that this is a debate with universal or world-historical significance or that its conclusions have anything more than heuristic value elsewhere. Everyone in the world today can learn from this particular engagement with difference, but they won't learn enough unless they are familiar with many other engagements.

A final note: my own familiarity with other engagements is limited, like everyone else's. The argument of this essay is worked mostly through examples from Europe, North America, and the Middle East. I will have to rely on other people to tell me whether, or to what extent, the argument fits Latin American, African, and Asian realities.

CHAPTER ONE

Personal Attitudes
and
Political Arrangements

Always begin negatively, a former teacher once instructed me. Tell your readers what you are not going to do; it will relieve their minds, and they will be more inclined to accept what seems a modest project. So I will begin this plea for tolerance with a couple of negative distinctions. I am not going to focus on the toleration of eccentric or dissident individuals in civil society or even in the state. Individual rights may well lie at the root of every sort of toleration, but I am interested in those rights primarily when they are exercised in common (in the course of voluntary association, religious worship, cultural expression, or communal self-government) or when they are claimed by groups on behalf of their members. The eccentric individual, solitary in his difference, is fairly easy to tolerate, and at the same time social repugnance for and resistance to eccentricity, although certainly unattractive, isn't terribly dangerous. The stakes are much higher when we turn to eccentric and dissident groups.

I am also not going to focus here on political toleration, where the groups in question are oppositional movements and parties. These are competitors for political power, and they are necessary in democratic regimes, which quite literally require that there be alternative leaders (with alternative programs), even if they never actually win an election. They are fellow participants, like the members of the opposing team in a basketball game, without whom there couldn't be a game, and who therefore have a right to score baskets and win, if they can. Problems arise only in the case of people who want to disrupt or stop the game while still claiming the rights of players and the protection of the rules. These problems are often hard, but they don't have much to do with the toleration of difference, which is intrinsic to democratic politics; rather they have to do with the toleration of disruption (or the risk of disruption), another matter entirely.

Nor is it intolerant of difference to ban a programmatically antidemocratic party from participating in democratic elections; it is merely prudent. Questions of toleration arise much earlier, before power is at stake, when the religious community or ideological movement out of which this party comes is first formed. At that stage, its members simply live among us, illiberally or antidemocratically different. Should we tolerate their preachings and practices, and if so (as I believe), how far should this toleration extend?

My concern, then, is with toleration when the differences at issue are cultural, religious, and way-of-life differences—when the others are not fellow participants and when there is no common game and no intrinsic need for the differences they cultivate and enact. Even a liberal society doesn't require a multiplicity of ethnic groups or religious communities. Its existence, even its flourishing, is entirely compatible with cultural homogeneity. Against this last claim, however, it has recently been argued that the liberal ideal of individual autonomy can only be realized in a "multicultural" society, where the presence of different cultures allows for meaningful choice.[1] But autonomous individuals can choose as well among jobs and professions; among potential friends and marriage partners; among political doctrines, parties, and movements; among urban, suburban, and rural living patterns; among high-brow, middle-brow, and low-brow cultural forms; and so on. There seems no reason why autonomy cannot find room enough within a single cultural group.

Nor do groups of this sort require, as democratic political parties do, that there be other groups of the same sort. Where pluralism is a social fact, as it commonly is, some of the groups will compete with others by seeking converts or supporters among uncommitted or loosely committed individuals. But their primary aim is to sustain a way of life among their own members, to reproduce their culture or faith in successive generations. They are in the first instance inwardly focused, which is exactly what political parties cannot be. At the same time, they require some kind of extended social space (outside the household) for the sake of assembly, worship, argument, celebration, mutual aid, schooling, and so on.

Now, what does it mean to tolerate groups of this sort? Understood as an attitude or state of mind, toleration describes a number of possibilities. The first of these, which reflects the origins of religious toleration in the sixteenth and seventeenth centuries, is simply a resigned acceptance of difference for the sake of peace. People kill one another for years and years, and then, mercifully, exhaustion sets in, and we call this toleration.[2] But we can trace a continuum of more substantive acceptances. A second possible attitude is passive, relaxed, benignly indifferent to difference: "It takes all kinds to make a world." A third follows from a kind of moral stoicism: a principled recognition that the "others" have rights even if they exercise those rights in unattractive ways.[3] A fourth expresses openness to the others; curiosity; perhaps even respect, a willingness to listen and learn. And, furthest along the continuum, there is the enthusiastic endorsement of difference: an aesthetic endorsement, if difference is taken to represent in cultural form the largeness and diversity of God's creation or of the natural world; or a functional endorsement, if difference is viewed, as in the liberal multiculturalist argument, as a necessary condition of human flourishing, one that offers to individual men and women the choices that make their autonomy meaningful.[4]

But perhaps this last attitude falls outside my subject: how can I be said to tolerate what I in fact endorse? If I want the others to be here, in this society, among us, then I don't tolerate otherness—I support it. I don't, however, necessarily support this or that version of otherness. I might well prefer another other, one who is culturally or religiously closer to my own practices and beliefs (or, perhaps, more distant, exotic, posing no competitive threat). And in any pluralist society there will always be people, however well entrenched their own commitment to pluralism, for whom some particular difference—perhaps a form of worship, family arrangement, dietary rule, sexual practice, or dress code—is very hard to live with. Though they support the idea of difference, they tolerate the instantiated differences. But even people who don't experience this difficulty are properly called tolerant: they make room for men and women whose beliefs they don't adopt, whose practices they decline to imitate; they coexist with an otherness that, however much they approve of its presence in the world, is still something different from what they know, something alien and strange. I shall say of all people who are able to do that, without regard to their standing on the continuum of resignation, indifference, stoical acceptance, curiosity, and enthusiasm, that they possess the virtue of tolerance.

As we shall see, it is a feature of any successful regime of toleration that it does not depend on a particular form of this virtue; it does not require that all its participants stand at one point on the continuum. It may be the case that some regimes make do more easily with resignation, indifference, or stoicism, whereas others need to encourage curiosity or enthusiasm, but I do not in fact see any systematic tendencies along these lines. Even the difference between the more collectivist and the more individualist regimes isn't reflected in the attitudes they require. But isn't toleration more stable if people are further along on the continuum? Shouldn't the public schools, for example, try to move them along? In fact, any of these attitudes, strongly established, will stabilize toleration. The best educational program might well involve nothing more than a graphic description of religious or ethnic warfare. No doubt personal relations across cultural lines would be improved by moving people beyond the minimal tolerance that graphic descriptions of intolerance aim to produce, but this is true in all the regimes; political success doesn't depend on good personal relations in any of them. I shall have to ask at the end, however, whether these claims still hold for the emerging "postmodern" version of toleration.

For the moment, I shall treat all the social arrangements through which we incorporate difference, coexist with it, allow it a share of social space, as the institutionalized forms of an undifferentiated virtue. Historically (in the West), there have been five different political arrangements that make for toleration, five models of a tolerant society. I don't claim that the list is exhaustive, only that it includes the most important and interesting possibilities. Mixed regimes are also possible, obviously, but I want now to describe these five in some rough fashion, combining historical and ideal-typical accounts. Then I shall examine some mixed cases, look at the problems the different arrangements confront and, finally, say something about the social world and self-understanding of the men and women who tolerate one another today (insofar as they actually do that: toleration is always a precarious achievement). What exactly do we do when we tolerate difference?

CHAPTER TWO

Five Regimes of Toleration

Multinational Empires

The oldest arrangements are those of the great multinational empires—beginning, for our purposes, with Persia, Ptolemaic Egypt, and Rome. Here the various groups are constituted as autonomous or semi-autonomous communities that are political or legal as well as cultural or religious in character, and that rule themselves across a considerable range of their activities. The groups have no choice but to coexist with one another, for their interactions are governed by imperial bureaucrats in accordance with an imperial code, like the Roman jus gentium, which is designed to maintain some minimal fairness, as fairness is understood in the imperial center. Ordinarily, however, the bureaucrats don't interfere in the internal life of the autonomous communities for the sake of fairness or anything else—so long as taxes are paid and peace maintained. Hence they can be said to tolerate the different ways of life, and the imperial regime can be called a regime of toleration, whether or not the members of the different communities are tolerant of one another.

Under imperial rule, the members will, willy nilly, manifest tolerance in (most of) their everyday interactions, and some of them, perhaps, will learn to accept difference and come to stand somewhere on the continuum that I have described. But the survival of the different communities doesn't depend on this acceptance. It depends only on official toleration, which is sustained, mostly, for the sake of peace— though individual officials have been variously motivated, a few of them famously curious about difference or even enthusiastic in its defense.[1] These imperial bureaucrats are often accused of following a policy of "divide and rule," and sometimes indeed that is their policy. But it has to be remembered that they are not the authors of the divisions they exploit and that the people they rule may well want to be divided and ruled, if only for the sake of peace.

Imperial rule is historically the most successful way of incorporating difference and facilitating (requiring is more accurate) peaceful coexistence. But it isn't, or at least it never has been, a liberal or democratic way. Whatever the character of the different "autonomies," the incorporating regime is autocratic. I don't want to idealize this autocracy; it can be brutally repressive for the sake of maintaining its conquests—as the histories of Babylonia and Israel, Rome and Carthage, Spain and the Aztecs, and Russia and the Tatars amply demonstrate. But settled imperial rule is often tolerant—tolerant precisely because it is everywhere autocratic (not bound by the interests or prejudices of any of the conquered groups, equally distant from all of them). Roman proconsuls in Egypt or British regents in India, for all their prejudices and the endemic corruption of their regimes, probably ruled more evenhandedly than any local prince or tyrant was likely to do—in fact, more evenhandedly than local majorities today are likely to do.

Imperial autonomy tends to lock individuals into their communities and therefore into a singular ethnic or religious identity. It tolerates groups and their authority structures and customary practices, not (except in a few cosmopolitan centers and capital cities) free-floating men and women. The incorporated communities are not voluntary associations; they have not, historically, cultivated liberal values. Though there is some movement of individuals across their boundaries (converts and apostates, for example), the communities are mostly closed, enforcing one or another version of religious orthodoxy and sustaining a traditional way of life. So long as they are protected against the more severe forms of persecution and allowed to manage their own affairs, communities of this sort have extraordinary staying power. But they can be very severe toward deviant individuals, who are conceived as threats to their cohesiveness and sometimes to their very survival.

So lonely dissidents and heretics, cultural vagabonds, intermarried couples, and their children will flee to the imperial capital, which is likely to become as a result a fairly tolerant and liberal place (think of Rome, Baghdad, and imperial Vienna, or, better, Budapest)[2]—and the only place where social space is measured to an individual fit. Everyone else, including all the free spirits and potential dissidents who are unable to move because of economic constraint or familial responsibility, will live in homogeneous neighborhoods or districts, subject to the discipline of their own communities. They are tolerated collectively there, but they will not be welcome or even safe as individuals across whatever line separates them from the others. They can mix comfortably only in neutral space—the market, say, or the imperial courts and prisons. Still, they live most of the time in peace, one group alongside the other, respectful of cultural as well as geographic boundaries.

Ancient Alexandria provides a useful example of what we might think of as the imperial version of multiculturalism. The city was roughly one-third Greek, one-third Jewish, and one-third Egyptian, and during the years of Ptolemaic rule, the coexistence of these three communities seems to have been remarkably peaceful.[3] Later on, Roman officials intermittently favored their Greek subjects, perhaps on grounds of cultural affinity, or perhaps because of their superior political organization (only the Greeks were formally citizens), and this relaxation of imperial neutrality produced periods of bloody conflict in the city. Messianic movements among Alexandria's Jews, partly in response to Roman hostility, eventually brought multicultural coexistence to a bitter end. But the centuries of peace suggest the better possibilities of the imperial regime. It is interesting to note that though the communities remained legally and socially distinct, there was significant commercial and intellectual interaction among them—hence the Hellenistic version of Judaism that was produced, under the influence of Greek philosophers, by Alexandrian writers like Philo. The achievement is unimaginable except in this imperial setting.

The millet system of the Ottomans suggests another version of the imperial regime of toleration, one that was more fully developed and longer lasting.[4] In this case, the self-governing communities were purely religious in character, and because the Ottomans were themselves Muslim, they were by no means neutral among religions. The established religion of the empire was Islam, but three other religious communities—Greek Orthodox, Armenian Orthodox, and Jewish—were permitted to form autonomous organizations. These three were equal among themselves, without regard to their relative numerical strength. They were subject to the same restrictions vis-à-vis Muslims—with regard to dress, proselytizing, and intermarriage, for example—and were allowed the same legal control over their own members. The minority millets (the word means religious community) were subdivided along ethnic, linguistic, and regional lines, and some differences of religious practice were thereby incorporated into the system. But members had no rights of conscience or of association against their own community (and everyone had to be a member somewhere). There was, however, further toleration at the margins: thus, Karaite sectarians within Judaism were accorded fiscal independence, though not full millet status, by the Ottomans in the sixteenth century. Basically, again, the empire was accommodating toward groups but not toward individuals —unless the groups themselves opted for liberalism (as a Protestant millet, established late in the Ottoman period, apparently did.)

Today, all this is gone (the Soviet Union was the last of the empires): the autonomous institutions, the carefully preserved boundaries, the ethnically marked identity cards, the cosmopolitan capital cities, and the far-flung bureaucracies. Autonomy did not mean much at the end (which is one reason, perhaps, for imperial decline); its scope was greatly reduced by the effect of modern ideas about sovereignty and by totalizing ideologies uncongenial to the accommodation of difference. But ethnic and religious differences survived, and wherever they were territorially based, local agencies, which were more or less representative, retained some minimal functions and some symbolic authority. These they were able to convert very quickly, once the empires fell, into a kind of state machine driven by nationalist ideology and aimed at sovereign power—and opposed, often enough, by established local minorities, the great beneficiaries of the imperial regime and its last and most stalwart defenders. With sovereignty, of course, comes membership in international society, which is the most tolerant of all societies but, until very recently, not so easy to get into. I shall consider international society only briefly and incidentally in this essay, but it is important to recognize that most territorially based groups would prefer to be tolerated as distinct nation-states (or religious republics) with governments, armies, and borders—coexisting with other nation-states in mutual respect or, at least, under the rule of a common (even if rarely enforced) set of laws.

International Society

International society is an anomaly here because it is obviously not a domestic regime; some would say that it is not a regime at all but rather an anarchic and lawless condition. If that were true, the condition would be one of absolute toleration: anything goes, nothing is forbidden, for no one is authorized to forbid (or permit), even if many of the participants are eager to do so. In fact, international society is not anarchic; it is a very weak regime, but it is tolerant as a regime despite the intolerance of some of the states that make it up. All the groups that achieve statehood and all the practices that they permit (within limits that I will come to in a moment) are tolerated by the society of states. Toleration is an essential feature of sovereignty and an important reason for its desirability.

Sovereignty guarantees that no one on *that* side of the border can interfere with what is done on *this* side. The people over there may be resigned, indifferent, stoical, curious, or enthusiastic with regard to practices over here, and so may be disinclined to interfere. Or perhaps they accept the reciprocal logic of sovereignty: we won't worry about your practices if you don't worry about ours. Live and let live is a relatively easy maxim when the living is done on opposite sides of a clearly marked line. Or they may be actively hostile, eager to denounce their neighbor's culture and customs, but unprepared to pay the costs of interference. Given the nature of international society, the costs are likely to be high: they involve raising an army, crossing a border, killing and being killed.

Diplomats and statesmen commonly adopt the second of these attitudes. They accept the logic of sovereignty, but they can't simply look away from persons and practices that they find intolerable. They must negotiate with tyrants and murderers and, what is more pertinent to our subject, they must accommodate the interests of countries whose dominant culture or religion condones, for example, cruelty, oppression, misogyny, racism, slavery, or torture. When diplomats shake hands or break bread with tyrants, they are, as it were, wearing gloves; the actions have no moral significance. But the bargains they strike do have moral significance: they are acts of toleration. For the sake of peace or because they believe that cultural or religious reform must come from within, must be local work, they recognize the other country as a sovereign member of international society. They acknowledge its political independence and territorial integrity —which together constitute a much stronger version of the communal autonomy maintained in multinational empires.

Diplomatic arrangements and routines give us a sense of what might be called the formality of toleration. This formality has a place, though it is less visible, in domestic life, where we often coexist with groups with which we don't have and don't want to have close social relations. The co-existence is managed by civil servants who are also domestic diplomats. Civil servants have more authority than diplomats, of course, and so the coexistence that they manage is more constrained than that of sovereign states in international society.

But sovereignty also has limits, which are fixed most clearly by the legal doctrine of humanitarian intervention. Acts or practices that "shock the conscience of humankind" are, in principle, not tolerated.[5] Given the weak regime of international society, all that this means in practice is that any member state is entitled to use force to stop what is going on if what is going on is awful enough. The principles of political independence and territorial integrity do not protect barbarism. But no one is obligated to use force; the regime has no agents whose function it is to repress intolerable practices. Even in the face of obvious and extensive brutality, humanitarian intervention is entirely voluntary. The practices of the Khmer Rouge in Cambodia, to take an easy example, were morally and legally intolerable, and because the Vietnamese decided to invade the country and stop them, they were in fact not tolerated. But this happy coincidence between what is intolerable and what is not tolerated is uncommon. Humanitarian intolerance isn't usually sufficient to override the risks that intervention entails, and additional reasons for intervening—whether geopolitical, economic, or ideological—are only sometimes available.

One can imagine a more articulated set of limits on the toleration that comes with sovereignty: intolerable practices in sovereign states might be the occasion for economic sanctions by some or all of the members of international society. The enforcement of a partial embargo against South African apartheid is a useful if unusual example. Collective condemnation, breaks in cultural exchange, and active propaganda can also serve the purposes of humanitarian intolerance, though sanctions of this sort are rarely effective.[6] So we can say that international society is tolerant as a matter of principle, and then more tolerant, beyond its own principles, because of the weakness of its regime.

Consociations

Before I consider the nation-state as a possibly tolerant society, I want to turn briefly to a morally closer but not politically more likely heir to the multinational empire—the consociational or bi- or trinational state.[7] Examples like Belgium, Switzerland, Cyprus, Lebanon, and the stillborn Bosnia suggest both the range of possibility here and the imminence of disaster. Consociationalism is a heroic program because it aims to maintain imperial coexistence without the imperial bureaucrats and without the distance that made those bureaucrats more or less impartial rulers. Now the different groups are not tolerated by a single transcendent power; they have to tolerate one another and work out among themselves the terms of their coexistence.

The idea is attractive: a simple, unmediated concurrence of two or three communities (in practice, of their leaders and elites) that is freely negotiated between or among the parties. They agree to a constitutional arrangement, design institutions and divide offices, and strike a political bargain that protects their divergent interests. But the consociation is not entirely a free construction. Commonly, the communities have lived together (or, rather, alongside one another) for a very long time before they begin their formal negotiations. Perhaps they were initially united by imperial rule; perhaps they first came together in the struggle against that rule. But all these connections are preceded by proximity: coexistence on the ground, if not in the same villages, then along a frontier only roughly defined and easily crossed. These groups have talked and traded, fought and made peace at the most local levels—but always with an eye to the police or army of some foreign ruler. Now they must look only to each other.

This isn't impossible. Success is most likely when the consociation predates the appearance of strong nationalist movements and the ideological mobilization of the different communities. It is best negotiated by the elites of the old "autonomies," who are often genuinely respectful of one another, have a common interest in stability and peace (and, obviously, in the ongoing authority of elites), and are willing to share political power. But the arrangements the elites work out, which reflect the size and economic strength of the associated communities, are dependent thereafter on the stability of their social base. The consociation is predicated, say, on the constitutionally limited dominance of one of the parties or on their rough equality. Offices are divided, quotas established for the civil service, and public funds allocated—all on the basis of this limited dominance or rough equality. Given these understandings, each group lives in relative security, in accordance with its own customs, perhaps even its own customary law, and can speak its own language not only at home but also in its own public space. The old ways are undisturbed.

It is the fear of disturbance that breaks up consociations. Social or demographic change, let's say, shifts the base, alters the balance of size and strength, threatens the established pattern of dominance or equality, undermines the old understandings. Suddenly one of the parties looks dangerous to all the others. Mutual toleration depends on trust, not so much in each other's good will as in the institutional arrangements that guard against the effects of ill will. Now the established arrangements collapse, and the resulting insecurity makes toleration impossible. I can't live tolerantly alongside a dangerous other. What is the danger that I fear? That the consociation will be turned into an ordinary nation-state where I will be a member of the minority, looking to be tolerated by my former associates, who no longer require my toleration.

Lebanon is the obvious example of this sad collapse of consociational understandings; it has guided the description I have just given. But in Lebanon something more than social change was involved. In principle, the new Lebanese demography or the new economy should have led to a renegotiation of the old arrangements, a simple redivision of offices and public funds. But the ideological transformations that came with social change made this very difficult to achieve. Nationalist and religious zeal and its inevitable concomitants, distrust and fear, turned renegotiation into civil war (and brought the Syrians in as imperial peacemakers). Against this background, consociation is clearly recognizable as a pre-ideological regime. Toleration is not out of the question once nationalism and religion are in play, and consociation may still be its morally preferred form. In practice, however, the nation-state is now the more likely regime of toleration: one group, dominant throughout the country, shaping public life and tolerating a national or religious minority—rather than two or three groups, each secure in its own place, tolerating one another.

Nation-States

Most of the states that make up international society are nation-states. To call them that doesn't mean that they have nationally (or ethnically or religiously) homogeneous populations. Homogeneity is rare, if not nonexistent, in the world today. It means only that a single dominant group organizes the common life in a way that reflects its own history and culture and, if things go as intended, carries the history forward and sustains the culture. It is these intentions that determine the character of public education, the symbols and ceremonies of public life, the state calendar and the holidays it enjoins. Among histories and cultures, the nation-state is not neutral; its political apparatus is an engine for national reproduction. National groups seek statehood precisely in order to control the means of reproduction. Their members may hope for much more—they may harbor ambitions that range from political expansion and domination to economic growth and domestic flourishing. But what justifies their enterprise is the human passion for survival over time.

The state these members create can nonetheless, as liberal and democratic nation-states commonly do, tolerate minorities. This toleration takes different forms, though it rarely extends to the full autonomy of the old empires. Regional autonomy is especially difficult to implement, for then members of the dominant nation living in the region would be subjected to "alien" rule in their own country. Nor are corporatist arrangements common; the nation-state is itself a kind of cultural corporation and claims a monopoly on such arrangements within its borders.

Toleration in nation-states is commonly focused not on groups but on their individual participants, who are generally conceived stereotypically, first as citizens, then as members of this or that minority. As citizens, they have the same rights and obligations as everyone else and are expected to engage positively with the political culture of the majority; as members, they have the standard features of their "kind" and are allowed to form voluntary associations, organizations for mutual aid, private schools, cultural societies, publishing houses, and so on. They are not allowed to organize autonomously and exercise legal jurisdiction over their fellows. Minority religion, culture, and history are matters for what might be called the private collective—about which the public collective, the nation-state, is always suspicious. Any claim to act out minority culture in public is likely to produce anxiety among the majority (hence the controversy in France over the wearing of Muslim headdress in state schools). In principle, there is no coercion of individuals, but pressure to assimilate to the dominant nation, at least with regard to public practices, has been fairly common and, until recent times, fairly successful. When nineteenth-century German Jews described themselves as "German in the street, Jewish at home," they were aspiring to a nation-state norm that made privacy a condition of toleration.[8]

The politics of language is one key area where this norm is both enforced and challenged. For many nations, language is the key to unity. They were formed in part through a process of linguistic standardization, in the course of which regional dialects were forced to give way to the dialect of the center—though one or two sometimes managed to hold out, and thus became the focus of subnational or protonational resistance. The legacy of this history is a great reluctance to tolerate other languages in any role larger than familial communication or religious worship. Hence the majority nation commonly insists that national minorities learn and use its language in all their public transactions—when they vote, go to court, register a contract, and so on.

Minorities, if they are strong enough, and especially if they are territorially based, will seek the legitimation of their own languages in state schools, legal documents, and public signage. Sometimes, one of the minority languages is in fact recognized as a second official language; more often, it is sustained only in homes, churches, and private schools (or is slowly and painfully lost). At the same time, the dominant nation watches its own language being transformed by minority use. Academies of linguists struggle to sustain a "pure" version, or what they take to be a pure version, of the national language, but their fellow nationals are often surprisingly ready to accept minority or foreign usages. This too, I suppose, is a test of toleration.

There is less room for difference in nation-states, even liberal nation-states, than in multinational empires or consociations—far less, obviously, than in international society. Because the tolerated members of the minority group are also citizens, with rights and obligations, the practices of the group are more likely than in multinational empires to be subject to majority scrutiny. Patterns of discrimination and domination long accepted—or, at any rate, not resisted—within the group may not be acceptable after members are recognized as citizens (I will consider some examples in Chapter 4). But there is a double effect here, with which any theory of toleration must reckon: though the nation-state is less tolerant of groups, it may well force groups to be more tolerant of individuals. This second effect is a consequence of the (partial and incomplete) transformation of the groups into voluntary associations. As internal controls weaken, minorities can hold their members only if their doctrines are persuasive, their culture attractive, their organizations serviceable, and their sense of membership liberal and latitudinarian. In fact, there is an alternative strategy: a rigidly sectarian closure. But this offers hope only of saving a small remnant of true believers. For larger numbers, more open and looser arrangements are necessary. All such arrangements, however, pose a common danger: that the distinctiveness of the group and of its way of life will slowly be surrendered.

Despite these difficulties, a variety of significant differences, especially religious differences, have been successfully sustained in liberal and democratic nation-states. Minorities often, in fact, do fairly well in enacting and reproducing a common culture precisely because they are under pressure from the national majority. They organize themselves, both socially and psychologically, for resistance, making their families, neighborhoods, churches, and associations into a kind of homeland whose borders they work hard to defend. Individuals, of course, drift away, pass themselves off as members of the majority, slowly assimilate to majority lifestyles, or intermarry and raise children who have no memory or knowledge of the minority culture. But for most people, these self-transformations are too difficult, too painful, or too humiliating; they cling to their own identities and to similarly identified men and women.

National (more than religious) minorities are the groups most likely to find themselves at risk. If these groups are territorially concentrated—like the Hungarians in Romania, say—they will be suspected, perhaps rightly, of hoping for a state of their own or for incorporation into a neighboring state where their ethnic relatives hold sovereign power. The arbitrary processes of state formation regularly produce minorities located in this way, groups that are subject to these suspicions and very hard to tolerate. Perhaps the best thing to do is to pull in the borders and let them go, or to grant them a full measure of autonomy.[9] We tolerate the others by contracting our state so that they can live in social space shaped to their own needs. Alternative solutions are more likely, of course: linguistic recognition and a very limited degree of administrative devolution are fairly common, though these are often combined with efforts to settle members of the majority in politically sensitive border regions and with periodic campaigns of assimilation.

After World War I, an effort was made to guarantee the toleration of national minorities in the new (and radically heterogeneous) "nation states" of Eastern Europe. The guarantor was the League of Nations, and the guarantee was written into a series of minority or nationality treaties. Appropriately, these treaties ascribed rights to stereotypical individuals rather than to groups. Thus the Polish Minority Treaty deals with "Polish nationals who belong to racial, religious, or linguistic minorities." Nothing follows from such a designation about group autonomy or regional devolution or minority control of schools. Indeed, the guarantee of individual rights was itself chimerical: most of the new states asserted their sovereignty by ignoring (or annulling) the treaties, and the League was unable to enforce them.

But this failed effort is well worth repeating, perhaps with a more explicit recognition of what the stereotypical minority member has in common with his or her fellows. The United Nation's Covenant on Civil and Political Rights (1966) takes this further step: minority individuals "shall not be denied the right, in community with other members of their group, to enjoy their own culture, to possess and practice their own religion, or to use their own language." [10] Note that this wording still falls within the nation-state norm: no recognition is accorded to the group as a corporate body; individuals act "in community with"; only the national majority acts as a community.

In time of war, the loyalty of national minorities to the nation-state, whether or not the minorities are territorially concentrated or internationally recognized, will readily be called into doubt—even against all available evidence, as in the case of anti-Nazi German refugees in France during the first months of World War II. Once again, toleration fails when the others look dangerous, or when nationalist demagogues can make them look dangerous. The fate of Japanese-Americans a few years later makes the same point—their fellow Americans imitated, as it were, conventional nation-statehood. In fact, the Japanese were not, and are not, a national minority in the United States, at least not in the usual sense: where is the majority nation? American majorities are temporary in character and are differently constituted for different purposes and occasions (minorities are often temporary too, though race and slavery together make an exception; I shall consider the exception later on). It is a crucial feature of the nation-state, by contrast, that its majority is permanent. Toleration in nation-states has only one source, and it moves or doesn't move in only one direction. The case of the United States suggests a very different set of arrangements.

Immigrant Societies

The fifth model of coexistence and possible toleration is the immigrant society.[11] Now the members of the different groups have left their territorial base, their homeland, behind them; they have come individually or in families, one by one, to a new land and then dispersed across it. Though they arrive in waves, responding to similar political and economic pressures, they don't arrive in organized groups. They are not colonists, consciously planning to transplant their native culture to a new place. They cluster for comfort only in relatively small numbers, always intermixed with other, similar groups in cities, states, and regions. Hence no sort of territorial autonomy is possible. (Though Canada is an immigrant society, Quebec is an obvious exception here; its original settlers did come as colonists, not as immigrants, and were then conquered by the British. Another exception must be made for the Aboriginal peoples, who were also conquered. I will focus here primarily on the immigrants. On the Québecois and Aboriginals, see the section "Canada" in Chapter 3; on American blacks, imported as slaves, see the section "Class" in Chapter 4.)

If ethnic and religious groups are to sustain themselves, they must do so now as purely voluntary associations. This means that they are more at risk from the indifference of their own members than from the intolerance of the others. The state, once it is pried loose from the grip of the first immigrants, who imagined in every case that they were forming a nation-state of their own, is committed to none of the groups that make it up. It sustains the language of the first immigration and, subject to qualification, its political culture too, but so far as contemporary advantages go, the state is, in the current phrase (and in principle), neutral among the groups, tolerant of all of them, and autonomous in its purposes.

The state claims exclusive jurisdictional rights, regarding all its citizens as individuals rather than as members of groups. Hence the objects of toleration, strictly speaking, are individual choices and performances: acts of adhesion, participation in rituals of membership and worship, enactments of cultural difference, and so on. Individual men and women are encouraged to tolerate one another as individuals, to understand difference in each case as a personalized (rather than a stereotypical) version of group culture—which also means that the members of each group, if they are to display the virtue of tolerance, must accept each other's different versions. Soon there are many versions of each group's culture, and many different degrees of commitment to each. So toleration takes on a radically decentralized form: everyone has to tolerate everyone else.

No group in an immigrant society is allowed to organize itself coercively, to seize control of public space, or to monopolize public resources. Every form of corporatism is ruled out. In principle, the public schools teach the history and "civics" of the state, which is conceived to have no national but only a political identity. This principle is, of course, only slowly and imperfectly enforced. Since public schools were founded in the United States, for example, the schools have mostly taught what English-Americans conceived as their own history and culture—which extend back to Greece and Rome and include classical languages and literature. There was and still is considerable justification for this standard curriculum, even after the immigrations of the mid-nineteenth century (when Germans and Irish arrived) and the turn of the century (when Southern and Eastern European peoples came), for American political institutions are best understood against this background. In more recent times (and in the course of a third great immigration, which this time is largely non-European), efforts have been made to incorporate the history and culture of all the different groups, to ensure a kind of equal coverage and so to create "multicultural" schools. In fact, the West still dominates the curriculum almost everywhere.

Similarly, the state is supposed to be perfectly indifferent to group culture or equally supportive of all the groups—encouraging, for example, a kind of general religiosity, as in those train and bus advertisements of the 1950s that urged Americans to "attend the church of your choice." As this maxim suggests, neutrality is always a matter of degree. Some groups are in fact favored over others—in this case, groups with "churches" more or less like those of the first Protestant immigrants; but the others are still tolerated. Nor is church attendance or any other culturally specific practice turned into a condition of citizenship. It is relatively easy, then, and not at all humiliating, to escape one's own group and take on the reigning political identity (in this case, "American").

But many people in an immigrant society prefer a hyphenated or dual identity, one differentiated along cultural or political lines. The hyphen joining Italian-American, for example, symbolizes the acceptance of "Italianness" by other Americans, the recognition that "American" is a political identity without strong or specific cultural claims. The consequence, of course, is that "Italian" is a cultural identity without political claims. That is the only form in which Italianness is tolerated, and then Italian-Americans must sustain their own culture, if they can or as long as they can, privately, through the voluntary efforts and contributions of committed men and women. And this is the case, in principle, with every cultural and religious group, not only with minorities (but, again, there is no permanent majority).

Whether groups can sustain themselves under these conditions—without autonomy, without access to state power or official recognition, and without a territorial base or the fixed opposition of a permanent majority—is a question still to be answered. Religious communities, of both sectarian and "churchly" sorts, have not done badly in the United States until now. But one reason for their relative success might be the considerable intolerance that many of them have in fact encountered; intolerance often has, as I have already suggested, group-sustaining effects. Ethnic groups have done less well, though observers eager to write them off are almost certainly premature. These groups survive in what we might think of as a doubly hyphenated version: the culture of the group is, for example, American-Italian, which means that it takes on a heavily Americanized form and is transfigured into something quite distinct from Italian culture in the home country; and its politics is Italian-American, an ethnic adaptation of local political practices and styles. Consider the extent to which John Kennedy remained an Irish "pol," Walter Mondale is still a Norwegian social democrat, Mario Cuomo is still an Italian Christian Democratic intellectual-in-politics, and Jesse Jackson is still a black Baptist preacher—each of them in many ways similar to, but in these ways different from, the standard Anglo-American type.[12]

Whether these differences will survive into the next generation or the one after that is uncertain. Straightforward survival is perhaps unlikely. But that is not to say that the successors to these four exemplary figures, and to many others like them, will all be exactly alike. The forms of difference characteristic of immigrant societies are still emerging. We don't know how "different" difference will actually be. The toleration of individual choices and personalized versions of culture and religion constitutes the maximal (or the most intensive) regime of toleration. But it is radically unclear whether the long-term effect of this maximalism will be to foster or to dissolve group life.

The fear that soon the only objects of toleration will be eccentric individuals leads some groups (or their most committed members) to seek positive support from the state—in the form, say, of subsidies and matching grants for their schools and mutual aid organizations. Given the logic of multiculturalism, state support must be provided, if it is provided at all, on equal terms to every social group. In practice, however, some groups start with more resources than others, and then are much more capable of seizing whatever opportunities the state offers. So civil society is unevenly organized, with strong and weak groups working with very different rates of success to help and hold their members. Were the state to aim at equalizing the groups, it would have to undertake a considerable redistribution of resources and commit a considerable amount of public money. Toleration is, at least potentially, infinite in its extent; but the state can underwrite group life only within some set of political and financial limits.

Summary

It will be useful here to list the successive objects of toleration in the five regimes (I don't mean to suggest that they mark a progress; nor is the order in which I have presented them properly chronological). In the multinational empire as in international society, it is the group that is tolerated— whether its status is that of an autonomous community or of a sovereign state. Its laws, religious practices, judicial procedures, fiscal and distributive policies, educational programs, and family arrangements are all viewed as legitimate or permissible, subject only to minimal and rarely strictly enforced (or enforceable) limits. The case is similar in the consociation, but now a new feature is added: a common citizenship more effective than that of most empires, one that at least opens up the possibility of state interference in group practices for the sake of individual rights. In democratic consociations (such as Switzerland), this possibility is fully realized, but rights will not be effectively enforced in the many other cases where democracy is weak, where the central state exists by mere sufferance of the consociated groups and is mostly focused on holding them together.

Nation-state citizenship is more meaningful. Now the objects of toleration are individuals conceived both as citizens and as members of a particular minority. They are tolerated, so to speak, under their generic names. But membership in the genus (in contrast to citizenship in the state) is not required of these individuals; their groups exercise no coercive authority over them, and the state will intervene aggressively to protect them against any effort at coercion. Hence new options are made available: loose affiliation with the group, nonaffiliation with any group, or assimilation to the majority. In immigrant societies, these options are widened. Individuals are tolerated specifically as individuals under their proper names, and their choices are understood in personal rather than stereotypical terms. Now there arise personalized versions of group life, many different ways of being this or that, which other members of the group have to tolerate if only because they are tolerated by the society as a whole. Fundamentalist orthodoxy distinguishes itself by its refusal to take this general toleration as a reason for a more latitudinarian view of its own religious culture. Sometimes, its protagonists oppose the immigrant society's regime of toleration as a whole.

CHAPTER THREE

Complicated Cases

Every case is unique, as anyone whose case it is knows well. But I want to look now at three countries where the lack of fit with the categories developed in Chapter 2 is especially obvious. All three involve socially or constitutionally mixed regimes that are doubly or triply divided and thus require the simultaneous exercise of different kinds of toleration; they reflect the ordinary complexity of "real life" from which my categories are necessarily abstracted. I will then turn briefly to the European Community, which is altogether new not so much in its mixing of regimes as in its incorporation of them into a still-developing constitutional structure.

France

France makes for an especially useful case study because it is the classic nation-state and, at the same time, Europe's leading immigrant society; indeed, it is one of the world's leading immigrant societies. The extent of its immigration has been obscured by the extraordinary assimilative powers of

the French nation—so that one imagines France as a homogeneous society with a highly distinctive and singular culture.
Until very recently, the large numbers of immigrants from
the East and South (Poles, Russians, Jews, Italians, and North
Africans) never constituted themselves as organized national
minorities. They produced communal organizations of various sorts—publishing houses, a foreign language press, and
so on—but (except for small groups of political refugees who
did not plan to stay) they came together only for mutual
comfort and support in the context of a highly pressured and
very rapid assimilation into French politics and culture. Far
more than any other European country, France has been a
society of immigrants.[1] And yet it isn't a pluralist society—
or at least it doesn't think of itself, and it isn't thought of, as
a pluralist society.

The most likely explanation for this anomaly—the
physical presence and conceptual absence of cultural difference—lies in modern French history, above all in the
revolutionary construction of a republican nation-state. The
nationalism that was created in the course of a political
struggle against the Church and the ancien régime was political and populist in character; it exalted the people as a body
of citizens committed to a cause. Though the cause was
French as well as republican, this was not a Frenchness that
could be defined religiously, ethnically, or historically. One
became French in this new sense of the word by becoming
republican; at the height of the revolution, foreigners were
welcomed, as they have been at least intermittently over the
years since—so long as they learned the French language,
committed themselves to the republic, sent their children to
state schools, and celebrated Bastille Day.[2]

What immigrants were not supposed to do was to organize any sort of ethnic community alongside (and potentially

in conflict with) the community of citizens. The French hostility to strong secondary associations that differentiate and divide the citizens is anticipated in Rousseau's political theory and was first expressed, with absolute clarity, in the Legislative Assembly's debate (in 1791) over the emancipation of the Jews. Clermont-Tonnerre, a deputy of the center, spoke for the majority (which favored emancipation) when he declared: "One must refuse everything to the Jews as a nation, and give everything to the Jews as individuals."[3] Writing in 1944, Jean-Paul Sartre argued that this was still the position of the typical French "democrat." "His defense of the Jew saves the latter as a man and annihilates him as a Jew . . . leave[s] nothing in him . . . but the abstract subject of the rights of man and the rights of the citizen."[4] Individuals could be naturalized and assimilated; Frenchness was in this sense an expansive identity. But France as a republican nation-state could not tolerate—so Clermont-Tonnerre had insisted—"a nation within a nation."

The revolution thus established the French attitude toward all immigrant groups. It was of a piece with the early and consistent denial that Normans, Bretons, or Occitaneans constituted a genuine national minority. And it has to be said that French republicans, over the years, were remarkably successful in maintaining the unitary ideal of the revolution. Certainly, the immigrants assimilated more or less willingly and were happy to be able to call themselves French citizens. They aimed to be tolerated only as individuals—men and women who attended a synagogue, say, or spoke Polish at home, or read Russian poetry. They had, or they admitted to, no public ambitions as members of a separate minority.

This was the situation until the collapse of the overseas empire and the arrival in France of large numbers of North African Jews and much larger numbers of Muslim Arabs.

These groups, in part because of their size, and in part because of a changing ideological climate, began to test and then to challenge the republican ideal. They have cultures of their own that they want to preserve and reproduce; they are not as ready as their predecessors were to surrender their children to state schools devoted to Frenchification (unlike "Americanization," no such word is actually in use, so unselfconscious has the process been).[5] They want to be recognized as a group and to be allowed to act out their group identity in public. They want to be French citizens while living, as it were, alongside the French, and many of them are actively intolerant of fellow Jews or Arabs who aim at an old-style assimilation for themselves or their children.

The immediate result is an uneasy standoff between republican assimilationists (represented by the government, political parties of the left and right, the teachers' union, and so on) and the new immigrant groups (represented by elected or self-appointed leaders and militants). The republicans seek to maintain a universal and uniform community of citizens, and they are tolerant of religious and ethnic diversity only so long as it is maintained in private or familial settings—the classic nation-state norm. The new immigrants, or many of them, seek some version of multiculturalism, though they are mostly not ready for the American version, where each culture is itself diversely constituted and internally conflicted. Perhaps what they are really looking for is something like the millet system—the overseas empire reestablished at home.

Israel

Israel is an even more complex case than France, for it incorporates three of the four domestic regimes—and the fourth was once proposed for it. A faction of the Zionist movement in the 1930s and 1940s argued for an Arab-Jewish consociation, a binational state. This plan proved impossible in practice because the central issue in dispute between Jews and Arabs was immigration policy. It was not a question of how to organize a regime of toleration (Within what structures might Jews and Arabs most readily tolerate each other?) but of who should be the participants in the regime (How many Jews and Arabs were there going to be?). With regard to this latter question, the two groups could not find a common answer. The immigration issue was particularly urgent for the Jews during the 1930s and 1940s, and it provided the chief motive for the establishment of an independent Jewish state.

That state is obviously not a consociation. But it is deeply divided nonetheless, and it is divided in three different ways. First, contemporary Israel is a nation-state that was established by a classic nineteenth-century nationalist movement and that incorporates a substantial "national minority," the Palestinian Arabs. Members of the minority are citizens of the state, but they do not find their history or culture mirrored in its public life. Second, Israel is one of the successor states of the Ottoman empire (the succession mediated by the British empire), and it has retained the millet system for its various religious communities—Jewish, Muslim, and Christian—allowing them to run their own courts (for family law) and providing a partially differentiated set of educational programs. And, third, Israel's Jewish majority is a society of immigrants who are drawn from every part of a widely scattered diaspora—an "ingathering" of men and women who have in fact, despite their common Jewishness (which is itself sometimes subject to dispute), very different histories and cultures. The differences are sometimes ethnic, sometimes religious. They make for a segmented majority

that draws together only in the face of minority militance—
and not always then. Zionism is a strong nationalizing force,
but it has not had the assimilative powers of French republicanism.

Each of these brief descriptions is, as it were, standard
for the type; each regime—nation-state, empire, and immigrant society—looks roughly the way it looks when it
exists independently. But in practice, the three press upon
one another in complex ways and make for tensions and
conflicts beyond those inherent in each one separately.[6] The
millet system, for example, locks individuals into their religious communities, but these are not the natural or singular
communities of all the citizens—and especially not of Jewish immigrants from Western Europe, the Americas, and the
former Soviet Union, many of whom are radically secular-
ized or religious in their own fashion. They experience the
rabbinic courts as intolerant and oppressive, relics of some
ancien régime they never knew.

Somewhat similarly, the Arab minority experiences the
Jewish immigrants as an affront and a threat—not only because they reinforce its minority status, but also because
they dominate the political struggle for recognition and equal
treatment. In contrast to the Arabs, these immigrants expect
to find their history and culture mirrored in the public life
of the Jewish state, but in fact many of them don't. Given
their own diversity, they are led to demand a version of the
state neutrality or multiculturalism characteristic of immigrant societies—which was not what the Zionist founders
had in mind. But though these arrangements in principle
include the Arabs, in practice they often do not—or they include them only in a formal sense, so that Arab schools, for
example, do not receive their just proportion of state funds.[7]

The effort to make mutual toleration work in the immigrant (or Jewish) context takes precedence over the effort to make the Jewish state fully tolerant of its Arab minority. Of course, this precedence is reinforced by the international conflict between Israel and its Arab neighbors, but it also reflects the difficult coexistence of the different regimes.

Toleration is made harder in these circumstances by an uncertainty about its proper object: individuals or communities? And if the latter, should these communities be religious, national, or ethnic? Presumably the answers must be inclusive: all of the above. Were the international conflict to be resolved, toleration in this triply divided society might prove easier than in many cases of singular division—because it would move, as it were, in different directions and be mediated through different institutional structures. But this mediation presupposes a gradual revision of the structures, an adjustment of each to the others. What would this process require? Perhaps a multiplication of religious courts so as to reflect the actual divisions in the three communities. Perhaps some kind of local autonomy for Arab towns and villages. Perhaps a unified "civics" curriculum, which would teach the values of democracy, pluralism, and toleration and be imposed on all the different state-run schools—Arab and Jewish, secular and religious. The first of these suggestions would adjust the millet system to the immigrant society; the second would modify the nation-state in the interests of its national minority; the third would assert the claims of that same state in the style of the immigrant society—that is, in political or moral rather than national, religious, or ethnic terms. But it is equally easy to imagine Israel experiencing reiterated crises in each of its regimes—and also along the "borders" where they interact.

Canada

Canada is an immigrant society with several national minorities—the Aboriginal peoples and the French—that are also conquered nations. These minorities are not dispersed the way the immigrants are, and they have a very different history. Individual arrival doesn't figure in their collective memory; they tell a story, instead, of long-standing communal life. They aspire to sustain that life, and they fear that it is unsustainable in the loosely organized, highly mobile, individualist society of the immigrants. Even strong multiculturalist policies are not likely to help minorities of this sort, for all such policies encourage only "hyphenated" identities—that is, fragmented identities, with each individual negotiating the hyphen, constructing some sort of unity for him or herself. What these minorities want, by contrast, is an identity that is collectively negotiated. And for that they need a collective agent with substantial political authority.

For the Québecois, what is most important is to live in French—to sustain the language that is now their chief distinguishing mark. Their everyday life is not significantly different from that of other Canadians. The Aboriginal nations still possess their own distinctive culture—which extends across the whole range of social activities—as well as their own languages. Both these groups probably need some degree of autonomy within Canada (or independence from Canada) if they are to maintain themselves in their present form. Does toleration require that they be permitted to do that, or try to do that, by exercising political authority and using the coercive powers that the project would require? Why shouldn't they be asked to adapt themselves to the model of an immigrant society?

But neither the Aboriginals nor the Québecois are immigrants. They never accepted the cultural risks and losses that immigration entails. The French came as colonists; the Aboriginals are what their name implies, indigenous peoples, which is to say, colonists from an earlier age. Both the Aboriginals and the French were conquered in wars we would probably regard as unjust (though the French-British wars may have been unjust on both sides, because what was at issue was who would dominate the "Indians"). Given a history of this kind, some sort of autonomy seems entirely justified. It is not easy to work out, however, because doing so would require a constitutional arrangement that treats different people differently and establishes different regimes in different parts of the same country—in a country committed to the liberal principle of equality before the law.

The refusal of Canadians (so far) to provide a constitutionally secure "special status" for Quebec—the chief cause of secessionist politics in the province—derives from this commitment. Why should this province be treated differently from all the others? Why should its government be granted powers denied the others? I have already suggested a historical answer to these questions, an answer that is indeed confirmed by the terms of the capitulation of the French in 1760 and by the Quebec Act of 1776, which incorporated Quebec into the British empire. The incorporation followed the standard pattern of imperial multinationalism: it "guaranteed that the Roman Catholic religion, French language, seigneurial property system, and the customary laws and forms of government from the French period would continue until a legislature was established. The Quebec legislators could then alter these old forms as they saw fit."[8]

Can an arrangement like this be carried over into a liberal state and immigrant society, whose other constituent groups have no such "guarantees"? The question has no obvious answer. But toleration, when it is extended to groups that are really different, that have different histories and cultures, probably requires some kind of legal and political differentiation. The argument for what Charles Taylor has called "asymmetrical federalism" doesn't depend only on the history (or the treaties); it rests most concretely on the actually surviving differences and the desire of the people who, so to speak, carry those differences forward to continue to do that: to sustain their own culture and to be recognized as its embodied representatives.[9] The desire is clear; only the means are in dispute. The Québecois claim that without sufficient authority to enforce the everyday use of French, they will soon find themselves, given current rates of immigration and the pressure of English speakers in Canada as a whole, unable to sustain French as a public language. But they also claim that the enforcement itself can be held within liberal limits — that is, that toleration can be accorded to non-French speakers (this was also guaranteed by the Quebec Act) — without endangering the project as a whole. If this is so, Quebec would seem to be a theoretically unproblematic case, despite the practical difficulties that have so far prevented, and may yet scuttle, a constitutional settlement.

The case of the Aboriginal peoples is harder, for it isn't at all clear that their way of life can be sustained, even under conditions of autonomy, within liberal limits: it isn't historically a liberal way of life. Internally intolerant and illiberal groups (like most churches, say) can be tolerated in a liberal society insofar as they take the form of voluntary associations. But can they be tolerated as autonomous communities with coercive authority over their members? This latter kind of toleration was possible in the old empires because the members were not citizens (or, at least, not citizens in any strong sense of the term)—hence the traditional leaders of the Aboriginal peoples can also refer themselves to treaties dating from the imperial age. But Aboriginals today are Canadian citizens, and the authority of their communities is limited by the higher law of Canada—the 1981 Charter of Rights and Freedoms, for example. Constitutional rights are limits on any collectivity; their purpose is to empower individuals, and so they necessarily put the collective (in this case, the tribal) way of life at risk.

Aboriginal culture is tolerated as the culture of a distinctive community, or set of communities, whose survival is only a standing possibility: there can be no guarantees. The communities are legally established, with recognized institutions, legitimate leaders, and available resources, all of which improve the odds of survival but provide no effective barriers against individual alienation and escape. The situation of the Aboriginals is thus different from that of Jews, Baptists, Lithuanians, or any other religious or immigrant community, for none of these is established or recognized in the same fashion. Because of their conquest and long subordination, the Aboriginal peoples are given, and should be given, more legal and political room to organize and enact their ancient culture. But the room still has windows and doors; it can't be closed off from the larger society, so long as its inhabitants are also citizens. Any of them can decide to leave and live outside or to campaign inside against established leaders and practices—in the same way, now, as do Jews, Baptists, and Lithuanians. Aboriginal nations are tolerated as nations, but their members are, at the same time, tolerated as individuals who can revise or reject their national way of life. The two forms of toleration coexist, even though the details of the coexistence remain to be worked out, and its long-term viability is still uncertain.

The European Community

I take the European Community as an example of a union of nation-states that isn't an empire or a consociation but something different from both and perhaps new in the world. Because it is still taking shape, its constitutional arrangements still disputed and uncertain, my account will be largely speculative. What forms might toleration take in the envisioned union?

The European Community is not an empire, despite the charges of imperial ambition leveled against its officials in Brussels, because its constituent states will surrender only a part of their sovereign powers. Whatever the extent of the surrender turns out to be, the powers states retain will reach far beyond autonomy. And it isn't a consociation because of the number of states involved and, again, because of their near-sovereignty. Why isn't the Community then simply an alliance of sovereign states for some limited purpose? The long history of alliance politics, however, shows nothing quite like the economic coordination that its members intend. And there is another reason why this model doesn't fit—the "Social Charter" to which the members have agreed. As it stands, the charter's stipulations are fairly weak, though they do decree, in addition to minimal standards for wages and the length of the work week, "equality between men and women with regard to labor market opportunities and treatment at work."[10] These stipulations differ from similar ones in the international bill of rights promulgated by the United Nations: they aren't merely hortatory, but are meant to be enforced, even if the enforcement mechanism is at this moment unclear.

In fact, there already exists a European convention on human rights, one that has been judicially enforceable since the 1960s, and the Community's charter has now been added to that. Imagine the two combined and expanded to a full set of negative and positive rights (I won't speculate here on the precise contents of the set): there would then be—perhaps there are already—practices tolerated in the member states, features of their political culture or long-standing social or economic arrangements (like gender inequality), that would not be tolerated in the new Community. In some respects, as we will see, the European Community requires its members to be more tolerant, and tolerant in different ways, than they have been in the past. But the charter, as I have imagined it, would establish a set of limits, and because these limits would be expressed in the language of rights, they would presumably dominate over all other rules and practices. This dominance would have significant entailments: it would shift the focus of political debate from legislatures to courts and semi-judicial administrative agencies (as it has to some extent done in the United States); it would increase the amount of litigation; and, most important, it would enhance the relative power of individuals vis-à-vis the nation-states or the ethnic or religious groups to which they belong. Whereas the old empires tolerated different legal cultures, the new Community seems likely to establish (over time, and assuming its continued development) a single overarching law.

At the same time, however, every member state will be more heterogeneous than it ever was before, in two senses. First, the Community recognizes regions within states as legitimate objects of social and economic policy—and it is likely some day to recognize them as political subjects as well. This recognition will almost certainly enhance the position of territorially concentrated minorities like the Scots or the Basques (it has already raised their ambitions). But the long-term consequences of regionalism may well be countered by the second source of new heterogeneity—immigration—which will tend to break up regional ethnic concentrations. Community "citizens" already move across state frontiers much more freely than they did in the past, and they carry with them not only whatever newly transportable rights they have been granted, but also their old cultures and religions. Majority nations will thus soon find themselves living with minorities to whom they are not accustomed; established national minorities will find themselves challenged by new groups with new ideas about the arrangements that toleration requires. The more people move around, the more the Community as a whole will come to resemble an immigrant society, with a large number of geographically dispersed minorities who have no strong connection to a particular piece of territory.

The member states, of course, will still be nation-states; no one expects the Dutch or the Danes, say, to take in so many immigrants that they become a minority, one group among many, in their own country. Nonetheless, the states will be bound to tolerate newcomers (who won't all be "Europeans," because any immigrant naturalized in one member state is admissible to all the others), whom they have not chosen for admission. They will make their own peace with these newcomers and with their cultural and religious practices, family arrangements, and political values—subject, always, to the Social Charter (which may or may not produce a common regime of toleration, depending on its eventual extent and enforcement).

Similarly, the newcomers will make their own peace with the political culture of their new country. No doubt different groups will seek different arrangements; despite the individualizing pressures that are felt in all immigrant societies, some of them will certainly seek corporatist arrangements. But these are unlikely to be acceptable to the host states, except in highly modified versions adjusted to the basic nation-state pattern of the voluntary association. Nor will the Community's officials in Brussels or its judges in Strasbourg intervene on behalf of corporatism; at most, they will enforce individual rights. The resulting pattern is uncertain: individuals will identify with ethnic or religious groups and claim some sort of state recognition, but the groups will be precarious, themselves subject to transformation as the immigrants adjust to their new environment, assimilate, intermarry, and so on. The European Community seems likely to bring to all its member states the advantages and strains of multiculturalism.

CHAPTER FOUR

Practical Issues

Power

In ordinary speech, it is often said that toleration is always a relationship of inequality where the tolerated groups or individuals are cast in an inferior position. To tolerate someone else is an act of power; to be tolerated is an acceptance of weakness.[1] We should aim at something better than this combination, something beyond toleration, something like mutual respect. Once we have mapped out the five regimes, however, the story looks more complicated: mutual respect is one of the attitudes that makes for toleration—the most attractive attitude, perhaps, but not necessarily the most likely to develop or the most stable over time. Sometimes, indeed, toleration works best when relations of political superiority and inferiority are clearly marked and commonly recognized. This is most obviously the case in international society, where ambiguous power relations are one of the chief causes of war. The same proposition probably holds with regard to some domestic regimes, like the consociation, where uncertainty about the relative power of different groups may lead to political turmoil and even to civil war. In immigrant societies, by contrast, the same uncertainty works in an opposite way: if people are unsure where they stand vis-à-vis others, toleration is obviously the most rational policy. Even here, however, questions about political power regularly arise—though perhaps not the single big question, who rules over whom? Instead a series of smaller questions regularly pose themselves: Who is stronger most of the time? Who is more visible in public life? Who gets the larger share of resources? These questions (the big one too) can hardly be understood without reference to the discussions still to come in this chapter about class, gender, religion, and so on; but they can also be asked independently.

In multinational empires, power rests with the central bureaucrats. All the incorporated groups are encouraged to regard themselves as equally powerless, and hence incapable of coercing or persecuting their neighbors. Any local attempt at coercion will produce an appeal to the center. So Greeks and Turks, for example, lived peacefully side by side under Ottoman rule. Were they mutually respectful? Some of them probably were; some were not. But the character of their relationship did not depend on their mutual respect; it depended on their mutual subjection. When subjection isn't an experience shared equally by all the incorporated groups, toleration among them is less likely. If one group feels a special affinity with the imperial center and is able to form an alliance with its local representatives, then it will often try to dominate the others—like the Greeks did in Roman Alexandria. In the imperial case, power is most effective in promoting toleration when it is distant, neutral, and overwhelming.

In this form, imperial power is clearly most helpful to

local minorities, who tend therefore to be the most loyal supporters of the empire. The leaders of national libera-tion movements commonly express (and exploit) resent-ment toward these same minorities, who are identified now as collaborators with the imperialists. The transition from imperial province to independent nation-state is a critical moment in the history of toleration. Often minorities are harassed, attacked, and forced to leave—as in the case of the Indian traders and artisans of Uganda, who were driven into exile soon after the withdrawal of the British (and who mostly followed the latter to Britain, bringing the empire home, as it were, and creating a new diversity in the imperial center). Groups of this sort sometimes manage to turn them-selves into tolerated minorities, but the path is always hard, and the endpoint, even if it is successfully reached, probably represents a net loss of security and status for the minori-ties. This is one of the common costs of national liberation, though it can be avoided, or at least mitigated, if the new nation-state is liberal and democratic.

Consociation probably requires something like mutual respect at least among the leaders of the different groups—for the groups must not only coexist but also negotiate among themselves the terms of their coexistence. The nego-tiators, like diplomats in international society, have to ac-commodate each other's interests. When they can't or won't do that, as in Cyprus after the British departure, consociation will fail. But individual members of the different commu-nities need not accommodate each other, except when they meet and bargain in the marketplace. In fact, consociation is probably easiest when the communities don't have much to do with one another, when each of them is relatively self-sufficient and inwardly turned. Then power is expressed—populations counted and wealth put into play—only at the

federal level, where communal leaders argue about budget-
ary allocations and the composition of the civil service.

In nation-states, power rests with the majority nation,
which uses the state, as we have seen, for its own purposes. This is no necessary bar to mutuality among individuals; in fact, mutuality is likely to flourish in liberal democratic states. But minority groups are unequal by virtue of
their numbers and will be democratically overruled on most
matters of public culture. The majority tolerates cultural
difference in the same way that the government tolerates
political opposition—by establishing a regime of civil rights
and civil liberties and an independent judiciary to guarantee
its effectiveness. Minority groups then organize, assemble,
raise money, provide services for their members, and pub-
lish magazines and books; they sustain whatever institutions
they can afford and think they need. The stronger their internal life and the more differentiated their culture is from
that of the majority, the less they are likely to resent the absence from the public sphere of any representations of their
own beliefs and practices. If minority groups are weak, by
contrast, their individual members will come increasingly to
adopt the beliefs and practices of the majority, at least in
public, and often privately as well. It is the intermediate positions that generate tension and lead to constant skirmishing
over the symbolism of public life. The contemporary French
case, as I described it in Chapter 3, provides ample evidence
for the last of these possibilities.

The case is similar early on in the history of immigrant societies, when the first immigrants aspire to nation-
statehood. Successive waves of immigration produce what
is, in principle, a neutral state, the democratic version of imperial bureaucracy. This state takes over and sustains—for
how long no one can know—some of the practical arrange-

ments and some of the symbolism of its immediate predecessor. So each new immigrant group has to adjust to, even if it also transforms, the language and culture of the first group. But the state claims to be above the fray, with no interest in directing the course of these transformations. It addresses itself only to individuals and so creates, or tends over time to create, an open society in which everyone, as I have argued, is engaged in the practice of toleration. The much heralded move "beyond toleration" is presumably now possible. It remains unclear, however, whether significant group differences will remain to be respected once this move is made.

Class

Intolerance is commonly most virulent when differences of culture, ethnicity, or race coincide with class differences—when the members of minority groups are also economically subordinated. This subordination is least likely to occur in multinational empires, where each nation has its own full complement of social classes. Multinationalism commonly produces parallel hierarchies, even if the different nations do not share equally in the wealth of the empire. International society is marked by the same parallelism, and so the inequality of nations produces no toleration problems (whatever its other problems). State elites interact in ways determined entirely by differences of power, not of culture; and the elites of dominant states learn very quickly to respect previously "inferior" cultures when their political leaders suddenly appear in the council of nations with new wealth, say, or new weapons.

Ideally, consociations take the same form—the different communities, unequal within, are roughly equal partners in the country as a whole. But it often happens that one community that is culturally different is also economically subordinate. The Lebanese Shi'a provide a useful example — of not only this double differentiation but also the political disenfranchisement that is its common consequence. The process works the other way too: when government officials discriminate against the members of such a group, the hostility these members encounter in every other area of social life is legitimized and intensified. The worst jobs, the worst housing, the worst schools: this is their common lot. They constitute an ethnically or religiously marked lower class. They are tolerated in some minimal sense — allowed their own houses of worship, for example — but they are strictly on the receiving end of this toleration. Consociational equality, and the mutual recognition it is supposed to generate, are both undercut by class inequality.

National minorities in nation-states sometimes find themselves in a similar position, and sometimes for the same reasons. Whether the causal sequence starts from cultural stigma or economic or political weakness, it regularly encompasses all three of these. But it can also happen that relatively powerless national minorities, the Chinese in Java, say, are well-off economically (though never as well-off as demagogues rallying the majority against them suggest). Retreating empires often leave successful minorities dangerously exposed to the intolerance of the new rulers of the nation-state. This intolerance can take extreme forms — as we have seen in the example of the Indian settlers in Uganda. Visible prosperity is certain to put a national minority, especially a new national minority, at risk. Invisible poverty, by contrast, brings less danger but greater misery, making for radical non-recognition and a kind of automatic, unreflective discrimination. Consider the "invisible" men and women of minority groups (or lower castes) who provide society's streetcleaners, garbage collectors, dishwashers, hospital orderlies, and so on—whose presence is simply taken for granted and who are rarely looked in the eye or engaged in conversation by members of the majority.

Immigrant societies regularly include groups of this sort —the newest immigrants from poorer countries, for example, who bring their poverty with them. But long-lasting poverty and cultural stigma are less often the lot of immigrants (who are, after all, the paradigmatic members of an immigrant society) than of conquered indigenous peoples and coercively imported groups like the black slaves and their descendants in the Americas. Here the most radical kind of political subordination goes along with the most radical kind of economic subordination, with racial intolerance playing an important role in both cases. The combination of political weakness, poverty, and racial stigma poses enormously difficult problems for the regime of toleration that the immigrant society is supposed to be. Stigmatized groups usually do not have the resources to sustain a strong internal life, so they cannot function like a corporately organized religious community in an imperial setting (though conquered natives are sometimes allowed the legal forms of such a community) or like a territorially based national minority. Nor are their individual members allowed to make their own way, following in the upward bound footsteps of the immigrants. They form an anomalous caste at the very bottom of the class system.

Toleration is obviously compatible with inequality whenever the class system is reiterated, more or less similarly, in each of the different groups. But this compatibility disappears when the groups are also classes. An ethnic or religious group that constitutes society's lumpen proletariat or underclass is virtually certain to be the focus of extreme intolerance—not, indeed, of massacre or expulsion (for the members of such groups often play an economically useful role that no one else wants to take on), but of daily discrimination, rejection, and debasement. Other people are, no doubt, resigned to their presence, but this is not the kind of resignation that counts as tolerance because it goes along with a wish for their invisibility.[2] In principle, one could teach respect for people of the underclass and their roles— as well as a wider toleration for all sorts of people doing all kinds of work, including hard and dirty work. In practice, neither specific respect nor wider toleration is likely unless the connection between class and group is broken.

The purpose of affirmative action or reverse discrimination in the admission of students to universities, the selection of civil servants, and the allocation of government funds is to break this link between class and group. None of these efforts are egalitarian so far as individuals are concerned; individuals are merely moved up or down the hierarchy. Affirmative action is egalitarian only at the group level, where it aims to produce similar hierarchies by supplying the missing upper, professional, or middle class to the most subordinate groups. If the social profile of all the groups is more or less the same, cultural difference is more likely to be accepted. This proposition doesn't hold in cases of severe national conflict, but where pluralism already exists, as in consociations and immigrant societies, it seems plausible. At the same time, the experience of the United States suggests that privileging the members of subordinate groups, whatever its useful long-term consequences, reinforces intolerance in the short term. It causes real injustice to particular individuals (usually members of the next-most-subordinate groups), and it breeds politically dangerous resentments. It may well be the case, then, that wider tolerance in pluralist societies requires a wider egalitarianism. The key to success in these regimes of toleration may not be—or may not only be—the reiteration of hierarchy in each group, but also the reduction of hierarchy across the society as a whole.[3]

Gender

Questions about family arrangements, gender roles, and sexual behavior are among the most divisive in all contemporary societies. It is a mistake to think that the divisiveness is entirely new: polygamy, concubinage, ritual prostitution, the seclusion of women, circumcision, and homosexuality have been argued about for millennia. Cultures and religions have marked themselves off by their distinctive practices in these matters—and then have criticized the practices of the "others." But a virtually universal male domination set limits to what could be argued about (and who could join the argument). Today, widely accepted ideas about equality and human rights call those limits into question. Everything now is open to debate, and every culture and religion is subject to a new critical scrutiny. This sometimes makes for toleration but sometimes, obviously, for its opposite. The theoretical and practical line between the tolerable and the intolerable is most likely to be fought over and eventually drawn here, with reference to what I will call, summarily, questions of gender.

The great multinational empires commonly left these questions to their constituent communities. Gender was taken to be an inherently internal affair; it didn't, or it was not supposed to, involve any kind of communal interaction. Strange commercial customs were not tolerated in the common markets, but family law ("private" law) was left entirely to the traditional religious authorities or the (male) elders.

Customary practice was also in their hands; imperial officials were unlikely to intervene.

Consider the extraordinary reluctance with which the British finally, in 1829, banned the suttee (the self-immolation of a Hindu widow on her husband's funeral pyre) in their Indian states. For many years, the East India Company and then the British government tolerated the practice because of what a twentieth-century historian calls their "declared intention of respecting both Hindu and Muslim beliefs and allowing the free exercise of religious rights." Even Muslim rulers, who had, according to this same historian, no respect whatsoever for Hindu beliefs, made only sporadic and half-hearted efforts to suppress the practice.[4] Imperial toleration extends, then, as far as the suttee, which—given British accounts of what the practice actually involved—is pretty far.

It is at least conceivable that consociational arrangements might produce a similar toleration, if the power of the joined communities was in near balance and the leaders of one of them were strongly committed to this or that customary practice. A nation-state, however, where power is by definition unbalanced, would not tolerate customs like the suttee among a national or religious minority. Nor is toleration at that reach likely in an immigrant society, where each of the groups is a minority relative to all the others. The case of the Mormons in the United States suggests that deviant practices like polygamy won't be tolerated even when they are wholly internal, when they involve "only" domestic life. In these last two cases, the state grants equal citizenship to all its members—including Hindu widows and Mormon wives—and enforces a single law. There are no communal courts; the whole country is one jurisdiction within which state officials are bound to stop a suttee in progress in exactly the same way that they are bound to stop a suicide attempt if they possibly can. And if the suttee is coercively "assisted," as in fact it often was, the officials have to treat the coercion as murder; there are no religious or cultural excuses.

That, at least, is what follows from the nation-state and immigrant society models as I have described them. But reality sometimes lags behind—as with another ritual practice involving women's bodies: genital mutilation or, more neutrally, clitoridectomy and infibulation. These two operations are commonly performed on infant girls or young women in a large number of African countries, and because no one has suggested humanitarian intervention to stop them, we can say that they are tolerated in international society (tolerated at the state level, but actively opposed by a number of organizations working in international civil society). The operations are also performed in African immigrant communities in Europe and North America. They have been specifically outlawed in Sweden, Switzerland, and Great Britain, though without any serious effort to enforce the ban. In France, the classic nation-state (which is now also, as we have seen, an immigrant society), some 23,000 girls were said to be "at risk" in the mid-1980s. How many of these were actually operated on is unclear. But there have been a number of highly publicized trials (under a general law against mutilation) of the women who perform the operations and of the mothers of the girls. The women have been convicted, and their sentences then suspended. In effect, the practice (as of the mid-1990s) is condemned publicly but tolerated in fact.[5]

The argument for toleration has to do with "respecting cultural diversity"—a diversity conceived, as in the standard nation-state model, to follow from the choices of stereotypical members of a cultural community. Thus a 1989 petition against criminalizing what the French call "excision": "Demanding a penal sentence for a custom that does not threaten the republican order and that there is no reason not to assign to the sphere of private choice, like circumcision, would demonstrate an intolerance that can only create more human drama than it claims to avoid, and that manifests a singularly narrow conception of democracy."[6] As with the suttee, it is important to get the description right: clitoridectomy and infibulation "are comparable . . . not to the removal of the foreskin but to the removal of the penis,"[7] and it is hard to imagine circumcision in that form being treated as a matter of private choice. In any case, the infant girls are not volunteers. And the French state, one would think, owes them the protection of its laws: some of them are citizens, and most of them will be the mothers of citizens. They are in any case residents of France and future participants in the social and economic life of the country; and although they may remain wholly confined within the immigrant community, they also (this is the advantage of living in France) may not. With regard to individuals like that, toleration surely should not extend to ritual mutilation, any more than it does to ritual suicide. Cultural diversity at that extreme is only protected against interference when boundaries are much more firmly drawn than they are or can be drawn in nation states or immigrant societies.[8]

In other sorts of cases, where the moral values of the larger community—the national majority or the coalition of minorities—are not so directly challenged, the excuse of religious or cultural difference (and "private choice") may be accepted, diversity respected, and nonstandard gender practices tolerated. Thus the case of narrowly constituted or sectarian minorities like the American Amish or the Hasidim, to whom state authorities are sometimes ready to offer (or the courts to mediate) one or another compromise arrangement—the separation of the sexes in school buses and even in classrooms, for example.

But similar concessions won't so readily be offered to larger, more powerful (and more threatening) groups even in relatively minor cases—and the standing compromises can always be challenged by any sect or group member who claims her citizen rights. Imagine that an arrangement is worked out (as it surely should be) allowing Muslim girls in French public schools to wear their customary headdress.[9] This would be a compromise with the nation-state norm, one that would recognize the right of immigrant communities to a (modestly) multicultural public sphere. The laicist traditions of French education would continue to govern the school calendar and curriculum. Imagine now that a number of Muslim girls claim that they are being coerced by their families to wear the headdress and that the compromise arrangement facilitates this coercion. Then the compromise would have to be renegotiated. In the nation-state and the immigrant society, though not in the multinational empire, the right to be protected against coercion of this kind (as, more obviously, one would be protected against the far more severe coercion of clitoridectomy) would take precedence over the "family values" of the minority religion or culture.

These are matters of extraordinary sensitivity. The subordination of women—manifest in seclusion, bodily concealment, or actual mutilation—is not aimed solely at the enforcement of patriarchal property rights. It also has to do with cultural or religious reproduction, of which women are taken to be the most reliable agents. Historically, men have entered into the larger public life of armies, courts, assemblies, and markets; they are always potential agents of novelty and assimilation. Just as national culture is better

preserved in rural than in urban settings, so it is better preserved in private or domestic than in public settings—which
is to say, in the standard cases, among women rather than
among men. Tradition is transmitted in the lullabies that
mothers sing, the prayers they whisper, the clothing they
make, the food they cook, and the domestic rites and customs that they teach. Once women enter the public sphere,
how will this transmission be effected? It is because education is the first point of entry that questions like the wearing
of traditional headdress in public schools are so fiercely con-
tested.

This is the form the argument takes when a traditional
culture or religion encounters the nation-state or the immigrant society. "You are committed to tolerating our community and its practices," the traditionalists say. "Given that
commitment, you cannot deny us control over our children
(and particularly our female children)—else you are not in
fact tolerating us." Toleration implies a right to communal
reproduction. But this right, if it exists, comes into conflict
with the rights of individual citizens—which were once confined to men and were therefore not so dangerous, but are
now extended to women. It seems inevitable that individual
rights will win out in the long run, for equal citizenship is
the basic norm of both the nation-state and the immigrant
society. Communal reproduction will then be less certain or,
at least, it will be realized through processes that yield less
uniform results. Traditionalists will have to learn a toleration of their own—for different versions of their own culture
or religion. But before that lesson is learned, we can expect
a long series of "fundamentalist" reactions that are focused
most often on questions of gender.

The abortion wars in the United States today suggest
the character of this reactionary politics. From the funda-

mentalist side, the moral issue is whether society will tolerate the murder of infants in the womb. But the political issue, for both sides, has a different focus: who will control the sites of reproduction? The womb is only the first of these; home and school come next and are already, as we have seen, in dispute. What cultural differences will remain to be tolerated once these disputes have been resolved, as they eventually will be, in favor of female autonomy and gender equality? If the traditionalists are right, nothing will remain. But they are unlikely to be right. Gender equality will take different forms in different times and places, and even in the same time and place among different groups of people, and some of these forms will turn out to be consistent with cultural difference. It may even happen that men will play a larger role in sustaining and reproducing the cultures they claim to value.

Religion

Most people in the United States, in the West generally, believe that religious toleration is easy. They read about religious wars near to home (in Ireland and Bosnia) or far away (in the Middle East or Southeast Asia) with incomprehension. Religion in those places must be contaminated by ethnicity or nationalism, or it must take some extreme, fanatical, and therefore (as we understand things) unusual form. For haven't we proved that freedom of worship, voluntary association, and political neutrality work together to reduce the stakes of religious difference? Don't these tenets of American pluralism encourage mutual forbearance and make for a happy coexistence? We allow individuals to believe what they want to believe, to join freely with fellow believers, to attend the church of their choice—or to disbelieve what they want to disbelieve, to stay away from the church of their choice, and so on. What more could anyone want? Isn't this the model of a toleration regime?

In fact, of course, there are other actual or possible regimes: the millet system was specifically designed for religious communities, and consociations commonly bring together different religious or ethnic groups. But the toleration of individual believers, as this was first worked out in England in the seventeenth century and then carried across the Atlantic, is the dominant model today. And so it is necessary to look closely at some of its complications. I want to consider two issues of historical and contemporary importance: first, the persistence at the margins of modern nation-states and immigrant societies of religious groups that demand recognition for the group itself rather than for its individual members, and second, the persistence of demands for "religious" tolerance and intolerance that extend beyond association and worship to a great variety of other social practices.

One reason that toleration works so easily in countries like the United States is that the churches and congregations that individuals form, whatever their theological disagreements, are, mostly, very much like one another. Seventeenth-century toleration was first of all a mutual accommodation of Protestants. And in the United States, after an early effort to establish a "holy commonwealth" in Massachusetts, the expanding toleration regime tended to protestantize the groups that it included. American Catholics and Jews gradually came to look less and less like Catholics and Jews in other countries: communal control weakened; clerics spoke with less authority; individuals asserted their religious independence, drifted away from the community, and intermarried; fissiparous tendencies well known from the first days of the Reformation became a general feature of American religious life. Toleration accommodated difference, but it also produced among the different groups a pattern of accommodation to the Protestant model that made coexistence easier than it might have been.

Some groups, however, resisted—Protestant sects determined to escape the "dissidence of dissent" (the ground, so to speak, in which they had originally taken root) and orthodox factions within the traditional religious communities. I will continue to refer to the examples of each mentioned earlier: the American Amish and the Hasidim. The toleration regime accommodated these groups too, though only at the margins. It permitted them their isolation, and it compromised with them on critical questions like public schooling. The Amish, for example, were for a long time permitted to educate their children at home; when they were finally required, first by the state of Pennsylvania and then by the Supreme Court (with reference to a Wisconsin case), to send the children to public schools, they were allowed to withdraw them at an earlier age than that stipulated in the law.[10] In principle, what was tolerated was a series of individual choices, made in successive generations, to join the Amish congregations and to worship in the Amish manner. In practice, it was the Amish community as a whole and its coercive control of its own children (which was only partly mitigated by public schooling) that was, and is, the real object of toleration. For the sake of (this kind of) toleration, we allow Amish children to receive less of an education in citizenship than we require of American children generally. The arrangement is justified in part by the marginality of the Amish, and in part by their embrace of marginality: their deep commitment not to live anywhere except on the margins of American society and not to seek any influence beyond them. Other similarly marginal religious sects have maintained a similar control over their children largely unchallenged by the liberal state.

The most interesting feature of early American toleration was the exemption from military service of the members of certain Protestant sects well known for their pacifist convictions.[11] Today, conscientious objection is an individual right, though the sign of conscientiousness that the political authorities are most ready to recognize is membership in those same sects. In its origins, however, objection was effectively a group right. Indeed, claims of conscience over a wide range of social issues—the refusal of oaths, of jury service, of public schooling, of taxes; the demand for polygamous marriage, animal sacrifice, ritual drug use, and so on—gain whatever legitimacy they have, even today, because they are religious practices, features of a collective way of life. These practices would have no legitimacy at all if they were put forward on a purely individual basis, even if the individuals insisted that their understanding of what they ought to do, or not to do, was a co-knowledge (con-science) shared between each of them and his or her God.

Minority religious practices and prohibitions, beyond association and worship, are tolerated or not depending on their visibility or notoriety and the degree of outrage they arouse in the majority. A great variety of practical accommodations are available in both nation-states and immigrant societies. Men and women who tell the authorities that their religion requires them to do this or that may well be permitted to do it, even if no one else is, especially if they do it quietly. And communal leaders who tell the authorities that their coercive power is necessary to the survival of the community may well be permitted to exercise that power, subject to certain liberal constraints. But pressure is steady, if only intermittently forceful, toward the individualist model: the community conceived as a free assembly—entrances and exits open, with little claim and little capacity to shape the everyday life of the participants.

At the same time, this regime of toleration is under pressure in the contemporary United States from groups within the (Christian) majority who have no quarrel with the freedom of assembly or worship but fear the loss of social control. They are prepared to tolerate minority religions (they are advocates, therefore, of religious liberty), but they have no tolerance for personal liberty outside the house of worship. If sectarian communities aim to control the behavior of their own people, the more extreme members of religious majorities aim to control everyone's behavior—in the name of a supposedly common (Judeo-Christian, say) tradition, of "family values," or of their own certainties about what is right and wrong. This is surely an example of religious intolerance. It is a sign of the partial success of the regime of toleration, however, that antagonism is not directed against particular minority religions but rather against the ambience of freedom that the regime as a whole creates.

No doubt toleration flourishes in this ambience—and even reaches what I have described as its most intensive form—but religious toleration, at least, doesn't depend upon it. Extensive restrictions on personal freedom such as a ban on abortion, the censorship of books and magazines (or of texts in cyberspace), discrimination against homosexuals, the exclusion of women from certain occupations, and so on, even if they are the products of religious intolerance, are entirely compatible with religious toleration—that is, with the existence of many different churches and congregations whose members worship freely in many different ways. The contradiction is not between toleration and restriction; it lies deep within the idea of religious toleration itself, because virtually all the tolerated religions aim to restrict individual freedom, which is, for liberals at least, the foundation of the idea. Most religions are organized to control behavior. When we require them to give up this aim, or to give up the means necessary to its achievement, we are requiring a transformation whose end product we cannot yet describe.

Entirely free religious communities already exist, of course, but they don't seem satisfying to all, perhaps not even to most, believers. Hence the recurrence of sectarian and cultic religiosity and of fundamentalist theologies, which challenge the prevailing regime of toleration. Assuming that the challenges are overcome (the same assumption that I have made in previous sections), what then? What will be the staying power and organizational strength of a purely voluntary faith?

Education

Schools have already figured significantly in this essay—most particularly in the discussion of gender and cultural reproduction. But there is an important issue that I must address here (and again in the section on civil religion), which has to do with the reproduction of the regime of toleration itself. Doesn't the regime have to teach all of its children, whatever their group memberships, the value of its own constitutional arrangements and the virtues of its founders, heroes, and current leaders? And won't that teaching, which is more or less unitary in character, interfere with or at least compete with the socialization of children into the various cultural communities? The answer, of course, is affirmative in both cases. All domestic regimes have to teach their own values and virtues, and this teaching is certainly competitive with whatever else children are taught by their parents or in their communities. But the competition is or can be a useful lesson in (the difficulties of) mutual toleration. State teachers must tolerate, say, religious instruction outside of their schools, and the teachers of religion must tolerate state organized instruction in civics, political history, the natural sciences, and other secular subjects. The children presumably learn something about how toleration works in practice and —when creationists, for example, challenge state instruction in biology—something also about its inevitable strains.

Multinational empires make the most minimal demands on the educational process. Their political history, which consists mostly of wars of conquest, is unlikely to inspire feelings of loyalty in the conquered peoples, and so it is best left out of the official curriculum (it is more likely to figure in communal stories of heroism in defeat). Loyalty to the emperor, portrayed as emperor of all his peoples, is more often taught. The emperor, rather than the empire, is the focus of official education, for the latter often has a clear national character whereas the individual leaders can at least pretend to rise above their national origin. Sometimes, indeed, they aim at radical transcendence, deification, which frees them from any particularist identity. But it is nonetheless an example of religious intolerance when the deified emperor demands to be worshipped by his subjects—like those Roman rulers who tried to bring statues of themselves into the temple in Jerusalem. The school is a better venue for the imperial image, which can look benignly down upon children studying anything at all, in any language, under any local or communal auspices.

Consociations can also teach a minimalist curriculum, one that is focused on an often sanitized history of communal coexistence and cooperation and on the institutions through which these are realized. The longer the coexistence has lasted, the more likely it is that the common political identity will have taken on cultural content of its own—as Swiss identity clearly has done—and will have become fully competitive with the identities of the different communities. Still, what is taught, in principle at least, is a political history in which these communities have a recognized and equal place.

The case is very different, obviously, in nation-states with national minorities, where one community is privileged over all others. This kind of regime is far more centralized than are empires and consociations, and so it has a greater need (particularly if it is democratically organized) for citizens—men and women who are loyal, engaged, competent, and familiar with the style, as it were, of the dominant nation. State schools will aim to produce citizens of this kind. Thus Arabs in France, for example, will be taught to be loyal to the French state, engaged in French politics, competent in the practices and expressive modes of French political culture, and knowledgeable about French political history and institutional structures. By and large, Arab parents and children seem to accept these educational aims; they have sought, as we have seen, to assert their Arab or Muslim commitment only through the symbolism of dress, not to alter the curriculum. They are, or they seem to be, content to sustain their own culture in nonstate schools, in religious settings, and at home. But French citizenship is a weighty matter, with resonance far beyond the narrowly political sphere. Its integrative and assimilative power has been demonstrated over many years and must appear to many parents, if not to their children, as a cultural threat. The more countries like France become (like) immigrant societies, the more this threat will be resisted.

What form that resistance is likely to take can be seen in the curricular wars of an immigrant society like the United States. Here children are taught that they are individual citizens of a pluralist and tolerant society—where what is tolerated is their own choice of cultural membership and identity. Most of them, of course, are already identified, because of the "choices" of their parents or, as in the case of racial identities, because of their location in a social system of differentiation. But they are, as Americans, entitled to make further choices and required to tolerate the existing identities and the further choices of their fellows. This freedom and this toleration constitute what we can call American liberalism.

The schools teach children from all of America's ethnic, religious, and racial groups to be liberal in this sense, and so to be Americans—much as children in French schools are taught to be republican and therefore French. But American liberalism is culturally neutral in a way that French republicanism cannot be. This difference seems to fit the two political doctrines: republicanism, as Rousseau taught, requires a strong cultural base to sustain high levels of participation among the citizens; liberalism, which is less demanding, can allow more room for private life and cultural diversity. But such differences can easily be exaggerated.[12] Liberalism is also a substantive political culture that has its origins, at least, in Protestant and English history. The recognition that American schools in fact reflect this history, and can hardly be neutral with regard to it, has led some non-Protestant and non-English groups to call for a multicultural education—which presumably requires not the subtraction of the liberal story from the curriculum but the addition of other stories.

It is commonly and rightly said that the point of multiculturalism is to teach children about each other's culture, to bring the pluralism of the immigrant society into its classrooms. Whereas the earlier version of neutrality, which was conceived or misconceived as cultural avoidance, aimed to make all the children into Americans simply (which is to say as much like English Protestants as possible), multicultural-ism aims to recognize them as the hyphenated Americans they are and to lead them to understand and admire their own diversity. There is no reason to think that this under-standing or admiration stands in any tension with the re-quirements of liberal citizenship—though it is important to stress again that liberal citizenship is more relaxed than that of a republican nation-state.

But multiculturalism is also, sometimes, a program of a different sort, one aimed at using the state schools to strengthen threatened or devalued identities. The point isn't to teach other children what it means to be different in a certain way, but to teach children who are supposed to be different how to be different in the right way. Hence the program is illiberal, at least in the sense that it reinforces established or presumed identities and has nothing to do with mutuality or individual choice. It probably also entails some form of educational separation, as in the theory and practice of Afrocentrism, which is a way of providing for black children in the state schools what the Church pro-vides for Catholic children in private schools. Now pluralism exists only in the system as a whole, not in the experience of each child, and the state must step in to compel the vari-ous schools to teach, whatever else they teach, the values of American liberalism. The Catholic example suggests that an immigrant society can make do with this arrangement, at least as long as the bulk of its schoolchildren are in mixed classrooms. Whether liberal politics could be sustained if all children received some version (their "own" version) of a Catholic parochial or Afrocentric education is more doubtful. Success would then depend on the effects of education outside the school: the everyday experience of mass communication, work, and political activity.

Civil Religion

Think of what is taught in state schools about the values and virtues of the state itself as the secular revelation of a "civil religion" (the term is Rousseau's).[13] Except in the case of the deified emperor, this revelation is religious mostly by analogy, but the analogy is worth pursuing. For here, as the school example makes clear, is a "religion" that can't be separated from the state: it is the very creed of the state, crucial to its reproduction and stability over time. Civil religion consists of the full set of political doctrines, historical narratives, exemplary figures, celebratory occasions, and memorial rituals through which the state impresses itself on the minds of its members, especially its youngest or newest members. How can there be more than one such set for each state? Surely civil religions can tolerate each other only in international society, not within a single domestic regime.

In fact, however, civil religion often makes for intolerance in international society by encouraging parochial pride about life on this side of the border and suspicion or anxiety about life on the other side. Its domestic effects, by contrast, can be benign, because it provides everyone (on this side of the border) with a common basic identity and so makes subsequent differentiation less threatening. Certainly civil religion, like state education, is sometimes competitive with group membership: thus the case of French republicans and French Catholics in the nineteenth century—or of republicans and Muslims today. But because civil religions commonly have no theology, they can also be accommodating of difference, even or especially of religious difference. Despite the specific historical conflict of the revolutionary years, then, there is no reason why a believing Catholic cannot also be a committed republican.

Toleration is most likely to work well when the civil religion is least like a . . . religion. Had Robespierre, for example, succeeded in binding republican politics to a fully elaborated deism, he might well have created a permanent barrier between republicans and Catholics (and Muslims, and Jews). But his failure is emblematic: political creeds take on the baggage of genuine religious belief at their peril. One might say the same thing about the baggage of genuine antireligious belief. Militant atheism made the communist regimes of Eastern Europe as intolerant as any other orthodoxy would have done—and politically weak as a result: they were unable to incorporate large numbers of their own citizens. Most civil religions wisely make do with a vague, unelaborated, latitudinarian religiosity, one that is more a matter of stories and holidays than of clear or firm beliefs.

Of course, it may be just this latitudinarianism that orthodox religious groups object to, fearing that it will make their children tolerant of religious error or secular disbelief. It is hard to know how to respond to anxieties of that sort; one hopes that they are justified and that the public schools and the stories and holidays of the civil religion will have exactly the effects that orthodox parents fear. Parents are free to pull their children out of the public schools and to escape the civil religion through one or another form of sectarian isolation. But it makes no sense to argue that respect for diversity bars an immigrant society like the United States from teaching respect for diversity. And it is certainly a legitimate form of such a liberal education to tell stories about the history of diversity and to celebrate its great occasions.[14]

In nation-states, the stories and celebrations will be of a different sort: they will come out of, and teach the value of, the historical experience of the majority nation. So the civil religion makes further differentiation possible within the majority—along religious, regional, and class lines—but provides no bridge to minority groups. Instead, it sets the standard for individual assimilation: it suggests, for example, that to become French you have to be able to imagine that your ancestors stormed the Bastille or, at least, that they would have done so had they been in Paris at the right time. But a national minority with a civil religion of its own can still be tolerated, so long as the rites are celebrated privately. And its members can become citizens, can learn the ways of, say, French political culture, without any imaginative investment in Frenchness.

The common identity fostered by a civil religion is especially important in immigrant societies where identities are otherwise so diverse. In multinational empires, obviously, identities are even more diverse, but there, beyond the unifying figure of the emperor and the common allegiance he claims, commonality is less important. Contemporary immigrant societies are also democratic states, and they are dependent for their political health on some degree, at least, of commitment and activism among their citizens. But if the local civil religion is to enhance and celebrate these qualities, it must accommodate not only other religions but also other civil religions. Its most enthusiastic protagonists, of course, will want to replace the others: that was the point, for example, of the Americanization campaigns of the early twentieth century. And perhaps, indeed, that will be the long-term effect of the American experience. Perhaps every immigrant society is a nation-state in the making, and civil religion is one of the instruments of this transformation.

Nonetheless, a campaign on its behalf is an act of intolerance, an act likely to provoke resistance and to multiply divisions among (and also within) the different groups.

It turns out, in any case, that a civil religion like Americanism can live fairly comfortably with what might be called alternative civil religious practices among its own participants. The stories and celebrations that go along with, for example, Thanksgiving, Memorial Day, or the Fourth of July can coexist in the common life of Irish-Americans, African-Americans, or Jewish-Americans with very different stories and celebrations. Difference here is not contradiction. Beliefs come into opposition far more readily than stories do, and one celebration doesn't deny, cancel, or refute another. Indeed, it is easier to watch the private communal or familial celebrations of our fellow citizens if we know that they will also be celebrating publicly with us on some other occasion. So civil religion facilitates the toleration of partial differences—or it encourages us to think of difference as only partial. We are Americans but also something else, and safe as something else insofar as we are Americans.

No doubt there are, or there might be, minority civil religions, ideologically or theologically elaborated, that contradict American values, but these have not been much in evidence in American public life. Similarly, it isn't difficult to imagine a more intolerant Americanism, one, for example, defined in Christian terms; connected exclusively, even racially, to its European origins; or given some narrow political content. Americanisms of this sort have existed in the past (hence the notion of "un-American activities" developed by the anticommunist right in the 1930s) and continue to exist, but none constitutes the dominant version right now. It isn't only in principle but also in reality that American society is a collection of individuals with multiple, partial identities. Of course, religions have often involved denials of such realities, and civil religions can attempt a similar denial. It may even be true that the pattern of difference in the United States and in other immigrant societies is unstable and impermanent. Even so, a Kulturkampf against difference is not the best response to this condition. Civil religion is more likely to succeed by accommodating than by opposing the multiple identities of the men and women it aims to engage. Its object, after all, is not full-scale conversion but only political socialization.

Tolerating the Intolerant

Should we tolerate the intolerant? This question is often described as the central and most difficult issue in the theory of toleration. But that can't be right, because most of the groups that are tolerated in all four domestic regimes are in fact intolerant. There are significant "others" about whom they are neither enthusiastic nor curious, whose rights they don't recognize—to whose existence, indeed, they are neither indifferent nor resigned. In multinational empires, the different "nations" are perhaps temporarily resigned; they accommodate themselves to coexistence under imperial rule. But were they to rule themselves, they would have no reason for resignation, and some of them certainly would aim at ending the old coexistence in one way or another. That might be a good reason for denying them political power, but it is no reason at all for refusing to tolerate them in the empire. The case is the same in consociations, where the whole point of the constitutional arrangement is to restrain the likely intolerance of the associated communities.

Similarly, minorities in nation-states and immigrant societies are and ought to be tolerated even if it is known that

their compatriots or fellow believers in power in other countries are brutally intolerant. These same minorities cannot
practice intolerance here (in France, say, or in America), that
is, they cannot harass their neighbors or persecute or repress
deviant or heretical individuals in their midst. But they are
free to excommunicate or ostracize deviants and heretics, and
they are equally free to believe and say that such people will
be damned forever or denied a place in the world to come—
or that any other group of their fellow citizens are living a life
that God rejects or that is utterly incompatible with human
flourishing. Indeed, many of the Protestant sectarians for
whom the modern regime of toleration was first designed,
and who made it work, believed and said just such things.

The point of separating church and state in the modern
regimes is to deny political power to all religious authorities, on the realistic assumption that all of them are at least
potentially intolerant. Given the effectiveness of the denial,
they may learn tolerance; more likely, they will learn to
live as if they possessed this virtue. Many more ordinary
believers obviously do possess it, especially in immigrant
societies, where daily encounters with both internal and ex-
ternal "others" are unavoidable. But these people too need
separation, and they are likely to support it politically as a
way of protecting themselves, and everyone else, against the
possible fanaticism of their fellow believers. The same possibility of fanaticism also exists among ethnic activists and
militants (in immigrant societies), and so ethnicity too has
to be separated from the state, for exactly the same reasons.

Democracy requires yet one more separation, one that
is not well understood: that of politics itself from the state.
Political parties compete for power and struggle to enact a
program that is, let's say, shaped by an ideology. But the win-
ning party, though it can turn its ideology into a set of laws,

cannot turn it into the official creed of the civil religion; it cannot make the day of its ascension to power into a national holiday, insist that party history be a required course in the public schools, or use state power to ban the publications or the assemblies of other parties.[15] That is what happens in totalitarian regimes, and it is exactly analogous to the political establishment of a single monolithic church. Religions that hope for establishment and parties that dream of total control can be tolerated both in liberal democratic nation-states and in immigrant societies, and they commonly are. But (as I suggested at the beginning of this essay) they can also be barred from seizing state power, and even from competing for it.[16] What separation means in their case is that they are confined to civil society: they can preach and write and meet; they are permitted only a sectarian existence.

CHAPTER FIVE

Modern and Postmodern Toleration

The Modern Projects

I have explored some of the limits of toleration, but I haven't yet discussed regimes of intolerance, which is what many empires, nation-states, and immigrant societies actually are. In these regimes, the toleration of difference is replaced by a drive toward unity and singularity. The imperial center aims to create something more like a nation-state: thus the "Russification" campaigns of nineteenth-century czars. Or the nation-state intensifies pressure on minorities and immigrants: assimilate or leave! Or the immigrant society heats up its "melting pot," looking to forge a new nationality (usually shaped in the mold of some earlier settler or immigrant group). "Americanization" in the United States in the early twentieth century is the example I have used for this latter project, which is in fact an effort to bring in immigrants without incorporating difference.

Efforts of this sort sometimes succeed in obliterating cultural and religious differences, but sometimes, when they

stop short of severe persecution, they serve in fact to reinforce them. They mark off the members of minority
groups, discriminate against them because of their membership, compel them to rely on one another, forge intense soli-
darities. Nonetheless, neither the leaders of such minority
groups nor their most committed members would choose a
regime of intolerance.[1] Given the opportunity, they will seek
some form of individual or collective toleration: assimilation
one by one into the body of citizens or recognition for their
group in domestic or international society, with a degree of
self-rule—regional or functional autonomy, consociation, or
sovereign statehood.

We might think of these two forms of toleration—individual assimilation and group recognition—as the central
projects of modern democratic politics. They are standardly
conceived in mutually exclusive terms: either individuals or
groups will be liberated from persecution and invisibility,
and individuals will be liberated only insofar as they abandon
their groups. I have already quoted Sartre's account of this
latter position, which has its origin in the French Revolution.
The revolutionaries aimed first to free the individual from
the old corporate communities and to establish him (and,
later, her) within a circle of rights—and then they aimed to
teach these rights-bearing men (and women) their citizenly
duties. Between the individual and the political regime, the
republic of French citizens, there was (in the minds of the
revolutionaries) only empty space, which facilitated easy
movement from private to public life and so encouraged cultural assimilation and political participation.

Postrevolutionary liberals and democrats slowly came
to value the intermediate associations that actually fill this
space, both as expressions of individual interests and beliefs and as schools of democracy. But these same associa-

tions also provide a kind of home for national minorities, where collective identity can be cultivated and pressures to assimilate resisted. And liberal democrats can accept both the cultivation and the resistance, within limits, until that point (whose location is always disputed) where the associations threaten to repress individual members or diminish their republican commitment. Republican citizens tolerate minority individuals by including them, whatever their religion or ethnicity, as fellow citizens, and then by tolerating the groups they form—insofar as these are, in the strongest sense of the term, secondary associations.

Democratic inclusiveness is the first modernist project. We can imagine the politics of the democratic left over the last two centuries as a series of struggles for inclusion: Jews, workers, women, blacks, and immigrants of many different kinds storm and breach the walls of the bourgeois city. In the course of the struggle, they form strong parties and movements, organizations for collective defense and advancement. But when they enter the city, they enter as individuals.

The alternative to entry is separation. This is the second modernist project: to provide the group as a whole with a voice, a place, and a politics of its own. Now what is required is not a struggle for inclusion but a struggle for boundaries. The crucial slogan of this struggle is "self-determination," which implies the need for a piece of territory or at least a set of independent institutions—hence, decentralization, devolution, autonomy, partition, or sovereignty. Getting the boundaries right, in not only geographic but also functional terms, is enormously difficult. Every political resolution is bitterly disputed. But there must be some resolution if the different groups are to exercise significant control over their own destiny and to do so with some security.

The work goes on today: adapting the old imperial ar-

rangements and extending the modern international system, proliferating nation-states, self-governing regions, distinct societies, local authorities, and so on. Note what is
being recognized and tolerated in this second project: it is
always groups and their members, men and women conceived to have singular or at least primary identities that
are ethnic or religious in character. The work obviously depends upon the mobilization of these people, but it is only
their leaders who are actually engaged with one another,
across boundaries, one on one (except when the engagement
is military in nature). Communal autonomy confirms the
authority of traditional elites; consociation commonly takes
the form of a power-sharing arrangement among those same
elites; nation-states interact through their diplomatic corps
and political leaders. For the mass of group members, toleration is maintained by separation, on the assumption that
these people understand themselves as members and want to
associate mostly with one another. They believe that "good
fences make good neighbors."[2]

But these two projects can also be pursued simultaneously by different groups or even by different members of
the same group. This latter possibility is in fact commonly
realized: some people seek escape from the confines of their
religious or ethnic membership, claiming to be citizens only,
whereas others want to be recognized and tolerated precisely as members of an organized community of religious
believers or ethnic relatives. Strong-willed (or simply eccentric) individuals who have broken loose from their communal backgrounds coexist with committed (or simply settled)
men and women who constitute the background and seek
to bring it forward. Then the two projects seem competitive with one another: should we prefer individual escape or
group commitment? There is no good reason, however, for

a fixed preference. The tension has to be worked out case by case, differently for different groups in different regimes (we have already looked at a number of examples). There is no overcoming this tension, for what would individuals escape from if group commitment collapsed? What kind of pride could they take in an escape that was never resisted? And who would they be if they did not have to struggle to become what they are? The coexistence of strong groups and free individuals, with all of its difficulties, is an enduring feature of modernity.

Postmodernity?

The last of my toleration models, however, points toward a different pattern and, perhaps, a postmodern project. In immigrant societies (and also now in nation-states under immigrant pressure), people have begun to experience what we might think of as a life without clear boundaries and without secure or singular identities. Difference is, as it were, dispersed, so that it is encountered everywhere, every day. Individuals escape from their parochial entanglements and mix freely with members of the majority, but they don't necessarily assimilate to a common identity. The hold of groups on their members is looser than it has ever been, but it is by no means broken entirely. The result is a constant commingling of ambiguously identified individuals, intermarriage among them, and hence a highly intensive multiculturalism that is instantiated not only in the society as a whole but also in a growing number of families, even in a growing number of individuals. Now tolerance begins at home, where we often have to make ethnic, religious, and cultural peace with our spouses, in-laws, and children—and with our own hyphenated or divided selves.

This kind of tolerance is especially problematic in the first generation of mixed families and divided selves when everyone still remembers, and perhaps longs for, more coherent communities and a more unified consciousness. Fundamentalism represents that longing in ideological form; its intolerance is focused, as I have already argued, not on other orthodoxies so much as on secular confusion and anarchy. Even for people who have no fundamentalist inclinations, however, the close-up encounter with difference may be disturbing. For many of them are still loyal to or at least nostalgic for the groups with which they, their parents, and their grandparents (on one side or the other) have historical connections.

Imagine now, some generations down the postmodern road, men and women entirely cut off from any such ties, fashioning their own "selves" out of the fragmentary remains of old cultures and religions (and anything else that may be available). The associations that these self-made and self-making individuals form are likely to be little more than temporary alliances that can be easily broken off when something more promising presents itself. Won't tolerance and intolerance in such a setting be replaced by mere personal liking and disliking? Won't the old public arguments and political conflicts about who to tolerate and how far to tolerate them be replaced by private melodramas? In this perspective, it is hard to see a future for any of the regimes of toleration. We will respond, I suppose, with resignation, indifference, stoicism, curiosity, and enthusiasm to the tics and foibles of our postmodern fellows. But because these fellows—these others—will not appear in recognizable sets, our responses will have no steady pattern.

The postmodern project undercuts every sort of common identity and standard behavior: it makes for a society

in which the plural pronouns "us" and "them" (and even
the mixed pronouns "us" and "me") have no fixed reference; it points to the very perfection of individual liberty.
The Bulgarian-French writer Julia Kristeva has been one of
the more interesting theoretical defenders of this project;
she urges us to recognize a world of strangers ("for only
strangeness is universal") and to acknowledge the stranger
in ourselves. In addition to a psychological argument, which
I must pass by here, she restates a very old moral argument
whose first version is the biblical injunction "Do not oppress
the stranger, for you were strangers in the land of Egypt."
Kristeva changes the pronoun, the verb tense, and the geog-
raphy for the sake of a contemporary reiteration: do not oppress the stranger, for we are all strangers in this very land.
Surely it is easier to tolerate otherness if we acknowledge the
other in ourselves.[3]

But if everyone is a stranger, then no one is. For unless
we experience sameness in some strong form, we cannot
even recognize otherness. A fellowship of strangers would
be at most a momentary grouping, existing only in opposition to some standing community. If there were no such
community, there would be no such fellowship. It is possible to imagine state officials "tolerating" all the postmodern
strangers; the criminal code would set the limits of toleration, and nothing more would be necessary. But the politics
of difference, the ongoing negotiation of group relations and
individual rights, would effectively have been abolished.

Kristeva tries to describe a nation-state that is on the
way, as it were, to this condition; she uses France (insofar as
it lives up to its Enlightenment heritage) as an example of
its "optimal rendition"—which makes her one of those ideal
immigrants who has a more principled patriotism than most
of the native-born ever reach. France at its best, Kristeva

writes, is a "transitional" society where national traditions are still "tenacious," but individuals can, to some degree at least, determine their own identities and create their own social groupings "through lucidity rather than fate." And this self-determination points toward a "still unforeseeable," but obviously imaginable, "polyvalent community . . . a world without foreigners"—which must also mean a France without the French (so Kristeva is, perhaps, only a temporary patriot).[4]

Even the most advanced immigrant societies—where self-fashioned individuals and individualized versions of culture and religion have made a considerably stronger appearance than in France—are not yet "polyvalent communities." We are still in that first generation: we don't live in the world of strangers all the time, nor do we encounter each other's strangeness only one on one. Instead we still experience difference collectively, in situations where personal relations must be seconded by the politics of toleration. It is not the case that the postmodern project simply supersedes modernism, as in some grand metanarrative of historical stages. The one is superimposed on the other, without in any way obliterating it. There still are boundaries, but they are blurred by all the crossings. We still know ourselves to be this or that, but the knowledge is uncertain, for we are also this *and* that. Groups with strong identities exist and assert themselves politically, but the allegiance of their members is measured by degrees along a broad continuum, with larger and larger numbers clustered at the farther end (which is why the militants at the near end are so strident these days).

This dualism of the modern and the postmodern requires that difference be doubly accommodated: first in its singular individual and collective versions and then in its pluralist, dispersed, and divided versions. We need to be tol-

erated and protected as citizens of the state and members
of groups—and also as strangers to both. Self-determination
has to be simultaneously political and personal—the two are
related, but they are not the same. The old understanding
of difference, which ties individuals to their autonomous or
sovereign groups, will be resisted by dissident and ambiva-
lent individuals. But any new understanding that is focused
solely on the dissidents will be resisted by men and women
still struggling to absorb, enact, elaborate, revise, and pass
on a common religious or cultural tradition. So, for now at
least, difference must be twice tolerated—on a personal as
well as a political level—with whatever mix (it doesn't have
to be the same mix in both cases) of resignation, indifference, stoicism, curiosity, and enthusiasm.

I am not sure, however, that these two versions of toleration are morally or politically equivalent. The divided
selves of postmodernity seem to be parasitic on the undi-
vided groups out of which they come, which form the cultural base, as it were, of their self-fashioning. What will
Kristeva's subjects be lucid about, if not their tenacious traditions? The farther they get from that cultural base, the
less they will have to work with. Isn't the postmodern
project, considered without its necessary historical background, likely to produce increasingly shallow individuals
and a radically diminished cultural life? There may be good
reasons, then, to live permanently with the problems of
what I have called the first generation. We should value the
extraordinary personal liberty that we enjoy as strangers
and possible strangers in contemporary "transitional" societies. But we need at the same time to shape the regimes of
toleration in ways that fortify the different groups and perhaps even encourage individuals to identify strongly with
one or more of them. Modernity requires, I have argued, an

enduring tension between individual and group, citizen and member. Postmodernity requires a similarly enduring tension with modernity itself: between citizens and members on the one hand and the divided self, the cultural stranger, on the other. Radical freedom is thin stuff unless it exists within a world that offers it significant resistance.

But if this is right, then my earlier claim that toleration works as well with any attitude on the continuum of resignation, indifference, stoicism, curiosity, and enthusiasm may have been falsified in our own time. It is only if groups are self-sustaining that resignation, indifference, or stoic acceptance will suffice for coexistence. That, indeed, has been the assumption of all the regimes: that religious, national, and ethnic groups are simply there, that they command strong loyalties that must, if anything, be modified to make room for patriotism and a common citizenship. But if groups are weak and need to be helped (as I will argue for the American case in the epilogue), then some mix of curiosity and enthusiasm is necessary. Nothing less will motivate the help they need. Free and fragmented individuals in democratic societies won't provide that help themselves, or authorize their governments to provide it, unless they recognize the importance of groups (their own and all the others) in the formation of individuals like themselves—unless they acknowledge that the point of toleration is not, and never was, to abolish "us" and "them" (and certainly not to abolish "me") but to ensure their continuing peaceful coexistence and interaction. The divided selves of postmodernity complicate that coexistence, but they also depend upon it for their own creation and self-understanding.

Reflections on American Multiculturalism

Two powerful centrifugal forces are at work in the United States today. One breaks loose whole groups of people from a presumptively common center; the other sends individuals flying off. Both these decentering, separatist movements have their critics, who argue that the first is driven by a narrow-minded chauvinism and the second by mere selfishness. The separated groups appear to these critics as exclusive and intolerant tribes, the separated individuals as rootless, lonely, and intolerable egotists. Neither of these views is entirely wrong, but neither is quite right. The two movements have to be considered together, set against the background of an immigrant society and a democratic politics that together allow these centrifugal forces to act. Understood in context, the two seem to me, despite the laws of physics, to be each the other's remedy.

The first of these forces is an increasingly strong articulation of group difference. It's the articulation that is new, obviously, because difference itself—pluralism, even multiculturalism—has been a feature of American life from very early on. John Jay, in one of the *Federalist Papers* (no. 2), describes the Americans as a people "descended from the same ancestors, speaking the same language, professing the same religion, attached to the same principles of government, very similar in manners and customs." These lines were already inaccurate when Jay wrote them in the 1780s, and they were utterly falsified in the course of the nineteenth century. Mass immigration turned the United States into a land of many different ancestors, languages, religions, manners and customs. Political principles, maxims of toleration: these constitute our only stable and common commitment. Democracy and liberty fix the limits and set the ground rules for American pluralism.

The contrasts that I have been making within the typology of regimes can help us grasp the radical character of this pluralism. Consider, first, the (relative) homogeneity of nation-states like France, Holland, Norway, Germany, Japan, and China, where, whatever regional differences exist, the great majority of the citizens share a single ethnic identity and celebrate a common history. And consider, second, the territorially based heterogeneity of the old multinational empires and then of the states that are their contemporary heirs—like the former Yugoslavia, the new Ethiopia, the new Russia, Nigeria, Iraq, India, and so on—where a number of ethnic and religious minorities claim ancient homelands (even if the boundaries are always in dispute). The United States differs from both these sets of countries: it isn't homogeneous nationally or locally; it's heterogeneous everywhere—a land of dispersed diversity that is (except for the remaining Native Americans) no one's homeland. Of course, there are local patterns of segregation, voluntary and involuntary; there are ethnic neighborhoods and places inexactly but evocatively called "ghettos." But none of our groups, with the partial and temporary exception of the Mormons in Utah, has ever achieved anything like stable geographical predominance. There is no American Slovenia, Quebec, or Kurdistan. Even in the most protected environments, Americans experience difference every day.

And yet the full-scale and fervent articulation of difference in the United States is a fairly recent phenomenon. A long history of prejudice, subordination, and fear worked against any public affirmation of minority "manners and customs" and so served to conceal the radical character of American pluralism. I want to be very clear about this history. At its extremes it was brutal, as conquered Native Americans and transported black slaves can testify; at its center, with regard to religion and ethnicity rather than race, it was relatively benign. An immigrant society welcomed new immigrants or at least made room for them, tolerated their beliefs and practices with a degree of reluctance considerably below the standards set elsewhere. Nonetheless, all our minorities learned to be quiet: timidity has been the mark of minority politics until recent times. The full realization of what it means to live among immigrants came very slowly.

I remember, for example, how in the 1930s and 1940s any sign of Jewish assertiveness—even the appearance of "too many" Jewish names among New Deal Democrats, union organizers, or socialist or communist intellectuals— was greeted among Jews with a collective shudder. The communal elders said, "Sha!" Don't make noise; don't attract attention; don't push yourself forward; don't say anything provocative. This was the way they understood the advice given by the prophet Jeremiah to the first Jewish exiles in Babylonia more than two millennia earlier and frequently repeated since: "Seek the peace of the city whither I have caused you to be carried away" (Jer. 29:7)—that is, be loyal to the powers that be and keep a low political profile. Jewish immigrants thought of themselves as exiles, guests of the (real) Americans, long after they had become American citizens.

Today all that is, as they say, history. The United States in the 1990s is socially, though not economically, a more egalitarian place than it was fifty or sixty years ago. The contrast between social and economic equality is very important, and I will come back to it; but let me focus now on the social side. No one is shushing us anymore; no one is intimidated or quiet. Old racial and religious identities have taken on greater prominence in our public life; gender and sexual preference have been added to the mix; and the current wave of immigration from Asia and Latin America makes for significant new differences among American citizens and potential citizens. And all this is expressed, so it seems, all the time. The voices are loud, the accents various, and the result is not harmony—as in the old image of pluralism as a symphony, with each group playing its own instrument (but who wrote the music?); the result is a jangling discord. It is very much like the dissidence of Protestant dissent in the early years of the Reformation, with many sects dividing and subdividing and many prophets and would-be prophets all talking at once. Hence the centrality of toleration as a political issue, manifest in the noisy arguments about political correctness, hate speech, multicultural curricula, first and second languages, immigration, and so on.

In response to this cacophony, another group of prophets—liberal and neoconservative intellectuals, academics, and journalists—wring their hands and assure us that the country is falling apart, that our fiercely articulated pluralism is dangerously divisive, and that we desperately need to reassert the hegemony of a single culture. Curiously, this supposedly necessary and necessarily singular culture is often described as a high culture, as if it is our shared commitment to Shakespeare, Dickens, and James Joyce that has been holding us together all these years. But surely high culture divides us, as it always has—and probably always will in any country with a strong egalitarian and populist strain. Doesn't anyone remember Richard Hofstadter's *Anti-Intellectualism in American Life?*[1] Political movements aimed at unity are more likely to invoke a vulgar and inauthentic nativism whose cultural content is certain to be low. These movements do not appeal to the literary or philosophical canon. But there is a better response to pluralism, it seems to me: democratic politics itself, where all the members of all the groups are (in principle) equal citizens who have not only to argue with one another but also, somehow, to come to an agreement. What they learn in the course of the necessary negotiations and compromises is probably more important than anything they might get from studying the canon. We need to think about how this practical, democratic learning can be advanced.

But isn't this learning already well advanced—given that multicultural conflicts take place in the democratic arena and require of their protagonists a wide range of characteristically democratic skills and performances? If one studies the history of ethnic, racial, and religious associations in the United States, one sees, I think, that they have served again and again as vehicles of individual and group integration—despite (or, perhaps, because of) the political conflicts they generated.[2] Even if the aim of associational life is to sustain difference, that aim has to be achieved under American conditions, and the result is commonly a new and unintended kind of differentiation. I have already cited one example of this phenomenon: the differentiation of American Catholics and Jews not so much from one another or from the Protestant majority as from Catholics and Jews in other countries. Minority groups adapt themselves to the local political culture: they become hyphenated Americans. And if their primary aim is self-defense, toleration, civil rights, a place in the sun, the result of their success is more clearly still an Americanization of whatever differences are being defended.

But the same thing happens to "nativist" or majority groups: they too are forced to adapt to an America filled with strangers. Imagining themselves as the original Americans, they too are slowly and painfully "Americanized." I don't mean to suggest that differences are quietly accepted or quietly defended. Quietness is not one of our political conventions; becoming an American often means learning not to be quiet. Nor is the success that is sought by one group always compatible with the success of all (or any of) the others. The conflicts are real, and even small-scale victories can be widely threatening. This is an important point: toleration brings an end to persecution and fearfulness, but it is not a formula for social harmony. The newly tolerated groups, insofar as they are really different, will often also be antagonistic, and they will seek political advantage.

The greater difficulties, however, come from disadvantage and failure, especially reiterated failure. It is associational weakness, and the anxieties and resentments it breeds, that pull people apart in dangerous ways and produce new forms of intolerance and bigotry—as in the more fierce and puritanical versions of "political correctness" and the more farfetched claims of ethnic and racial mythology. The noisiest groups in our contemporary cacophony, and the groups that make the most extreme demands, are also the weakest and the poorest. In American cities today, poor people, mostly members of minority groups, find it difficult to work together in any coherent way. Mutual assistance, cultural preservation, and self-defense are loudly affirmed but ineffectively enacted. The contemporary poor have no strongly based or well-funded institutions to focus their energies or to discipline wayward members. They are socially exposed and vulnerable.

What has happened in the United States these last decades is both unexpected and disturbing—but also, just possibly, in a way that I need to explain, heartening. The economic gap has widened even as the social gap has narrowed; inequalities of income and resources are greater today than they were a half century ago. But they do not consistently produce in the lower fourth or fifth of the social order the "appropriate" consciousness, the mental reflection of defeat: resignation and deference. There is no pervasive culture of compliance, no group of people morally prepared to be tractable and uncomplaining, like the "respectable poor" of—so it seems—long ago. Or if there are such people, they are, more than they ever were before, invisible—culturally as well as politically inarticulate and unrepresented. What we see is certainly depressing enough: a large number of disconnected, powerless, and often demoralized men and women who are spoken for, and also exploited by, a growing company of racial and religious demagogues and tinhorn charismatics. But at least these people are not silent, crushed, broken, so that one feels that some of them, at least, might be available for a more hopeful mobilization in a different political environment.

The political environment, however, is what it is, and it does not offer much short-term hope. Weakness is the general, if uneven, feature of associational life in today's America; any program for political renewal must start from this reality. Unions, churches, interest groups, ethnic organizations, political parties and sects, societies for self-improvement and good works, local philanthropies, neighborhood clubs and cooperatives, religious sodalities, brotherhoods and sisterhoods: American civil society is wonderfully multitudinous. Most of these associations, however, are precariously established, skimpily funded, and always at risk. They have less reach and holding power than they once did.[3] The number of Americans who are unorganized, inactive, and undefended (though still angry and noisy) is on the rise. Why is this so?

The answer has to do in part with the second of the centrifugal forces at work in contemporary American society. This country is not only a pluralism of groups but also a pluralism of individuals; its regime of toleration is focused, as we have seen, on personal choices and lifestyles rather than on common ways of life. It is perhaps the most individualist society in human history. Compared to the men and women of any earlier, old-world country, we are all radically liberated. We are free to plot our own course; to plan our own lives; to choose a career, a partner (or a succession of partners), a religion (or no religion), a politics (or an antipolitics), a lifestyle (any style)—we are free to "do our own thing." Personal freedom and the radical forms of toleration that go with it are certainly the most extraordinary achievements of the "new order of the ages" celebrated on the Great Seal of the United States. The defense of this freedom against puritans and bigots is one of the enduring themes of American politics and makes for its most zestful moments; the celebration of this freedom, and of the individuality and creativity it allows, is one of the enduring themes of our literature.

Nonetheless, personal freedom is not an unalloyed delight, for many Americans lack the means and the power to "do their own thing" or even to find their own things to do. Empowerment is more often a familial, class, or communal achievement than an individual one. Resources have to be accumulated, cooperatively, over generations. And without resources, individual men and women find themselves hard-pressed by economic dislocations, natural disasters, govern-mental failures, and personal crises. Many of them live every day with the frustrations of failure. They can't count on steady or significant familial or communal support. Often they are on the run from family, class, or community, seek-ing new lives and new identities in this new world. If they make good their escape, they never look back; if they need to look back, they are likely to find the people they left behind barely able to support themselves. These are the excitements of postmodernity, but they often make for a sad story—or, better, a series of similar but unrelated sad stories.

Consider for a moment the cultural (ethnic, racial, and religious) groups that constitute our supposedly fierce and divisive multiculturalism. All of these are voluntary associa-tions, with a core of militants, activists, and believers and a wide periphery of more passive men and women who are, in effect, cultural free-riders. These people claim an identity (or more than one) that they don't pay for with money, time, or energy. When they find themselves in trouble, they look for help from similarly identified men and women. But the help is uncertain, for these identities are mostly unearned, without depth. Footloose individuals are not reliable mem-bers. There are no borders around our cultural groups and, of course, no border police. Men and women are free to par-ticipate or not as they please, to come and go, to withdraw entirely, or simply to fade away into the peripheral distances. They are free to mix and mingle in the different cultures, to explore and challenge all the boundaries. This freedom, again, is one of the advantages of an immigrant society; at the same time, however, it doesn't make for strong or cohesive associations. Ultimately, I'm not sure that it makes for strong or self-confident individuals.

Rates of disengagement from cultural association and identity for the sake of the private pursuit of happiness (or the desperate search for economic survival) are so high these days that all the groups worry about how to hold the periphery and ensure their own future. They are constantly fund-raising; recruiting; scrambling for workers, allies, and endorsements; preaching against the dangers of assimilation, intermarriage, passing, or passivity. Lacking any sort of coercive power and unsure of their own persuasiveness, some of these groups demand governmental programs (targeted entitlements or quota systems) that will help them press their own members into line. From their perspective, the real alternative to multicultural toleration is not a strong and substantive Americanism (as if America were an old-world nation-state), but an empty or randomly filled individualism, a great drift of human flotsam and jetsam away from every creative center.

This is, again, a one-sided perspective on individual freedom in an immigrant society, but it isn't entirely wrongheaded. Despite appearances, the critical conflict in American life today is not between multiculturalism and some kind of cultural hegemony or singularity, not between pluralism and unity or the many and the one. We live instead with the peculiarly modernist and postmodernist conflict between the manyness of groups and of individuals. And this is a conflict in which we have no choice except to affirm the value of both sides. The two pluralisms make America what it is or sometimes is and set the pattern for what it should be. Taken together, but only together, they are entirely consistent with a common democratic citizenship.

Consider now the increasingly dissociated individuals of

contemporary American society. Surely we ought to worry about the processes that produce dissociation and are its products (even though these are also, some of them, emancipatory processes):[4]

- the high divorce rate, steadily rising until very recently, when it seems to have leveled off;
- the still rising number of children being raised by single, and often frighteningly young, mothers;
- the recent increase in reports of child abuse and abandonment;
- the growing number of people living alone (in what the census calls "single person households");
- the decline in memberships—in labor unions; in the older, more established churches (though evangelical churches and sects are on the rise); and in philanthropic societies, parent-teacher organizations, and neighborhood clubs;
- the long-term decline in voting rates and party loyalty (perhaps most dramatically demonstrated in local elections);
- the high rate of geographic mobility, which undercuts neighborhood cohesiveness;
- the sudden appearance of homeless men and women; and
- the rising tide of random violence.

The apparent stabilization of high levels of unemployment and underemployment among young people and minority groups intensifies all these processes and aggravates their effects. Unemployment makes family ties brittle, cuts people off from unions and interest groups, drains communal resources, leads to political alienation and withdrawal, and increases the temptation of a criminal life. The old maxim about idle hands and the devil's work isn't necessarily true, but it becomes true whenever idleness is a condition that no one would freely choose.

I am inclined to think that these processes, on balance, are more worrying than the multicultural cacophony—if only because, in a democratic society, action in common is better than withdrawal and solitude, tumult is better than passivity, and shared purposes (even when we don't approve) are better than private listlessness. It is probably true, moreover, that many of these dissociated individuals are available for far-right, ultranationalist, fundamentalist, or xenophobic mobilizations of a sort that democracies ought to avoid if they can. There are writers today, of course, who claim that multiculturalism is itself the product of such mobilizations: American society in their eyes stands at the brink not only of dissolution but also of "Bosnian" civil war.[5] In fact, we have had, so far, only intimations of an openly chauvinist and racist politics. More Americans are involved in weird religious cults than in far-right political groups (though these sometimes overlap). We are at a point where we can still safely bring the pluralism of groups to the rescue of the pluralism of dissociated individuals.

Individuals are stronger, more confident, more savvy, when they are participants in a common life, when they are responsible to and for other people. No doubt this relation doesn't hold for every common life; I am not recommending the weird religious cults—though even these have to be tolerated, within whatever limits are set by our ideas about citizenship and individual rights. Perhaps men and women who manage to pass through such groups will be strengthened by the experience, educated for a more modest commonality. For it is only in the context of associational activity that individuals learn to deliberate, argue, make decisions, and take responsibility. This is an old argument, first made on behalf of Protestant congregations and conventicles, which served, so we are told, as schools of democracy in nineteenth-century

Great Britain, despite the intense and exclusive bonds they created and their frequently expressed doubts about the salvation of nonbelievers.[6] Individuals were indeed saved by congregational membership—saved from isolation, loneliness, feelings of inferiority, habitual inaction, incompetence, and a kind of moral vacancy—and turned into useful citizens. It is equally true, of course, that Britain was saved from Protestant repression by the strong individualism of these same useful citizens: that was a large part of their usefulness.

But no regime of toleration can be built solely on such "strong" individuals, for they are the products of group life and won't, by themselves, reproduce the connections that made their own strength possible. So we need to sustain and enhance associational ties, even if these ties connect some of us to some others and not everyone to everyone else. There are many ways of doing this. First and foremost among them are government policies that create jobs and that sponsor and support unionization on the job. For unemployment is probably the most dangerous form of dissociation, and unions are not only training grounds for democratic politics but also instruments of "countervailing power" in the economy and of local solidarity and mutual aid.[7] Almost as important are programs that strengthen family life, not only in its conventional but also in its unconventional versions—in any version that produces stable relationships and networks of support.

But I want to focus again on cultural associations, because these are the ones thought to be so threatening today. It is the weakness of these associations, not their strength, it seems to me, that threatens our common life. One reason for the decline of unions in contemporary America is the virtual disappearance of a distinctive working-class culture—or, rather, of the set of working-class cultures (Irish, Italian,

Slavic, Scandinavian, and so on) that made labor radicalism possible in the late nineteenth and early twentieth centuries. Men and women need the ties that come with language and memory, with familiar rituals of celebration and mourning, with common practices, even with common games and songs, if they are to work together over a long period of time. Civil religion provides some of these ties for the citizens as a whole, but the vitality and discipline of an immigrant society depend on the more intense connections provided by its constituent groups. So we need more cultural associations, not fewer, and more powerful and cohesive ones, too, with a wider range of responsibilities.

Associations of this sort are not the objects of toleration in immigrant societies, but they can be made the objects— or better, the ends—of government policy. Consider, for example, the current set of federal programs—including tax exemptions, matching grants, subsidies, and entitlements— that enable religious communities to run their own hospitals, old age homes, schools, day care centers, and family services. Here are welfare societies within a decentralized (and still unfinished) American welfare state. Tax money is used to second charitable contributions in ways that reinforce the patterns of mutual assistance and cultural reproduction that arise spontaneously within civil society. But these patterns need to be greatly extended, because coverage at present is radically unequal. And more groups must be brought into the business of welfare provision: racial and ethnic as well as religious groups (and why not unions, co-ops, and corporations too?).

We also need to find other programs through which the government acts indirectly to support citizens acting directly in local communities: these might include "charter schools" designed and run by teachers and parents; tenant self-management and co-op buy-outs of public housing; experiments in workers' ownership and control of factories and companies; locally initiated building, clean-up, and crime prevention projects; and communally based museums, youth centers, radio stations, and athletic leagues. Programs like these will often create or enhance parochial communities, and they will generate conflicts over the state budget and local struggles for control of political space and institutional functions. Toleration, remember, is not a formula for harmony: it legitimates previously repressed or invisible groups and so enables them to compete for available resources. But the presence of these groups, in force, will also increase the amount of political space and the number and range of institutional functions and, therefore, the opportunities for individual participation. And participating individuals, with a growing sense of their own effectiveness, are our best protection against the parochialism and intolerance of the groups in which they participate.

Engaged men and women tend to be widely engaged —active in many different associations both locally and nationally. This is one of the most common findings of political scientists and sociologists (and one of the most surprising: where do these people find the time?).[8] It helps to explain why engagement works, in a pluralist society, to undercut racist or chauvinist political commitments and ideologies. The same people show up for union meetings, neighborhood projects, political canvassing, church committees, and—most reliably—in the voting booth on election day. They are, most of them, articulate, opinionated, skillful, sure of themselves, and fairly steady in their commitments. Some mysterious combination of responsibility, ambition, and meddlesomeness carries them from one meeting to another. Everyone complains (I mean all of them complain) that there are so few of them. Is their small number an inevitability of social life, so that an increase in associations would only stretch out the competent people more and more thinly? I suspect that demand-side economists have a better story to tell about this "human capital:" multiply the calls for competent people, and the people will appear. Multiply the opportunities for action in common, and activists will emerge to seize the opportunities. Some of them, no doubt, will be narrow-minded and bigoted, interested in nothing beyond the advancement of their own group, but the greater their number and the more diverse their activities, the less likely it is that narrow-mindedness and bigotry will prevail.

A certain sort of stridency is a feature of what we may one day come to recognize as *early* multiculturalism; it is especially evident among the newest and weakest, the poorest and least organized, groups, where economic deprivation goes hand in hand with minority status—where class is, not entirely but in large part, a function of race and culture. This stridency is the product of a historical period when the social equality promised (and, in part, delivered) by our regime of toleration is steadily being undercut by economic inequality.

Stronger organizations, capable of collecting resources and delivering real benefits to their members, will gradually move these groups toward mutual toleration and a democratically inclusive politics. No doubt there is a tension between members and citizens, between particular interests and the common interest, but there is also real continuity between them. Citizens committed to the common interest don't come out of nowhere. They are the members of groups that feel themselves to have a stake in the country as a whole, first of all in the regime of toleration itself and then in the broader politics of the regime. And so they look to participate in national decision-making.

Remember that this has happened before, in the course of ethnic and class conflict. When groups consolidate, the center holds the periphery and turns it into a political constituency. So union militants, say, begin on the picket line and the strike committee and move on to the school board and the city council. Or religious and ethnic activists begin by defending the interests of their own community and end up in political coalitions, fighting for a place on "balanced" tickets and talking (at least) about the common good. The cohesiveness of the group invigorates its members, and the ambition and mobility of the most vigorous members liberalizes the group.

Some of these members will flee their own groups, join others, or undertake complicated cross-cultural careers. They will seize on the possibilities of dissociation and commingling. They will act as radically free individuals, pursuing their own material or spiritual interests. But if they act against a background of group strength, they will also be agents of cultural innovation and mutual learning. Postmodern vagabonds, when they don't replace but live alongside members and citizens, are unlikely to find themselves talking only to themselves, endlessly self-absorbed; they will be participants in interesting conversations.

These conversations should take place everywhere, but perhaps especially in the public schools (and in public and private colleges and universities), which have historically been marked, at least in the major immigrant centers, by an integrative mode of association. Public schools bring together the children of parents committed to different religious and ethnic communities—as well as the children of parents who have escaped or are in the process of escaping from such commitments. Themselves supposedly neutral with reference to the communities and their escaped members, the schools ought to provide a sympathetic account of the history and philosophy of our own regime of toleration, which can hardly avoid specifying its particularist (English Protestant) origins. They ought to teach the American civil religion and aim to produce American citizens, and so they will inevitably challenge cultural communities where citizenship of that sort is unfamiliar.

Should public schools do more than this? Should they help children escape from such communities and wander on their own through the cultural world? Should they aim to produce more vagabonds? Certainly, it is tempting to imagine democratic education as a training in critical thought, so that the students can undertake an independent, preferably skeptical, evaluation of all established belief systems and cultural practices: for aren't critics the best citizens?[9] Maybe so; in any case we need more of them. And yet they may not be the most tolerant fellow citizens; they may not be resigned or indifferent to the parochial loyalties of their fellows—or even stoically accepting of them. Democracies need critics who possess the virtue of tolerance, which probably means critics who have loyalties of their own and some sense of the value of associational life. The schools can help meet this latter need simply by recognizing the plurality of cultures and by teaching something about the different groups (even uncritically: the experience of difference will itself encourage critical exchange). For the state system should also have a second aim, which is entirely compatible with the first: to produce hyphenated citizens, men and women who will defend toleration within their different communities while still valuing and reproducing (and rethinking and revising) the differences.

I don't mean to sound like the famous Pollyanna. These outcomes won't come about by chance; perhaps they won't come about at all. Everything is harder now—family, class, and community are less cohesive than they once were; governments and philanthropies command fewer resources; the street world of crime and drugs is more frightening; and individual men and women seem more adrift. There is one further difficulty that we ought, however, to welcome. In the past, organized groups have succeeded in entering the American mainstream only by leaving other groups (and the weakest of their own members) behind. And the men and women left behind commonly accepted their fate or at least failed to make much noise about it. Today, as I have argued, the level of resignation is considerably lower, and if much of the subsequent noise is incoherent and futile, it serves nonetheless to remind the rest of us that there is a larger social agenda than our own success. Multiculturalism as an ideology is a program for greater social and economic equality. No regime of toleration will work for long in an immigrant, pluralist, modern, and postmodern society without some combination of these two: a defense of group differences and an attack upon class differences.

If we want the mutual reinforcements of community and individuality to serve a common interest, we will have to act politically to make them effective. They require certain background or framing conditions that can only be provided by state action. Group life won't rescue individual men and women from dissociation and passivity unless there is a political strategy for mobilizing, organizing, and if necessary subsidizing the right sort of groups. And strong-minded individuals won't diversify their commitments and extend their ambitions unless there are opportunities—jobs, offices, and responsibilities—open to them in the larger world. The centrifugal forces of culture and selfhood will correct one another only if the correction is planned. It is necessary to aim at a balance of the two. This means that we can never be consistent defenders of multiculturalism or individualism; we can never be simply communitarians or liberals, or modernists or postmodernists, but must be now one, now the other, as the balance requires. It seems to me that the best name for the balance itself—the political creed that defends the framework, supports the necessary forms of state action, and so sustains the modern regimes of toleration—is social democracy. If multiculturalism today brings more trouble than hope, it does so in part because of the weakness of social democracy (in this country, left liberalism). But that is another, longer story.

Notes

INTRODUCTION: HOW TO WRITE ABOUT TOLERATION

1. I have written critically about this approach in "A Critique of Philosophical Conversation," in Michael Kelly, ed., *Hermeneutics and Critical Theory in Ethics and Politics* (Cambridge, Mass.: MIT Press, 1990), pp. 182–96. Cf. Georgia Warnke's "Reply," pp. 197–203 of this same book, which offers a partial defense of the theory of Jürgen Habermas.

2. Thomas Scanlon explains why sayings of this sort matter in "Contractualism and Utilitarianism," in Amartya Sen and Bernard Williams, eds., *Utilitarianism and Beyond* (Cambridge: Cambridge University Press, 1982). esp. p. 116.

3. Stuart Hampshire, *Morality and Conflict* (Cambridge, Mass.: Harvard University Press, 1983), pp. 146–48.

4. It may be useful if I list, early on, some of the contributions to this debate that have inspired my own: John Higham, *Strangers in the Land: Patterns of American Nativism 1860–1925,* 2d ed. (New Brunswick, N.J.: Rutgers University Press, 1988); Orlando Patterson, *Ethnic Chauvinism: The Reactionary Impulse* (New York: Stein and Day, 1977); Stephen Steinberg, *The Ethnic Myth: Race, Ethnicity, and Class in America* (Boston: Beacon, 1981); Arthur M. Schlesinger, Jr., *The Disuniting of America* (New York: Norton, 1992); David Hollinger, *Postethnic America* (New York: Basic Books, 1995); Todd Gitlin, *The Twilight of Common Dreams* (New York: Henry Holt, 1995); and Charles Taylor, *Multiculturalism and "the Politics of Recognition"* (Princeton, N.J.: Princeton University Press, 1994). Taylor is a near neighbor, and his defense of "deep diversity" in Canada has figured centrally in my own thinking about the United States.

CHAPTER 1: PERSONAL ATTITUDES AND POLITICAL ARRANGEMENTS

1. Joseph Raz, "Multiculturalism: A Liberal Perspective," in *Dissent* (winter 1994): 67–79.

2. This exhaustion, and the prudential calculations it allows, is best exemplified in the French *politiques* of the sixteenth century: see the brief account in Quentin Skinner, *The Foundations of Modern Political Thought,* vol. 2: *The Age of Reformation* (Cambridge: Cambridge University Press, 1978), pp. 249–54.

3. Many philosophers would restrict tolerance to this attitude alone, a view that corresponds to some uses of the word and catches a certain reluctance commonly ascribed to the practice of toleration. But this interpretation misses entirely the enthusiasm of many of the earliest advocates of toleration. See David Heyd, ed., *Toleration: An Elusive Virtue* (Princeton, N.J.: Princeton University Press, 1996), especially Heyd's introduction and the opening essay by Bernard Williams.

4. For a historical account that reveals all of these attitudes, see Wilbur K. Jordan, *The Development of Religious Toleration in England,* 4 vols. (Cambridge: Cambridge University Press, 1932–40).

CHAPTER 2: FIVE REGIMES OF TOLERATION

1. The earliest examples of what came to be the academic discipline of anthropology are the work of imperial officials: consider, for example, the career and writings of the Roman provincial administrator Tacitus as described by Moses Hadas in his introduction to *The Complete Works of Tacitus* (New York: Modern Library, 1942).

2. In fact, imperial cosmopolitanism was reproduced in much smaller cities, local centers such as Ruschuk (Ruse), the Danube port city in Bulgaria where Elias Canetti grew up. Under Ottoman rule, Ruschuk became a multicultural city, inhabited by Bulgarians, Jews, Greeks, Albanians, Armenians, and Gypsies. See Canetti's description in *The Tongue Set Free,* trans. Joachim Neugroschel (New York: Farrar, Straus and Giroux, 1979).

3. I rely here chiefly on P. M. Fraser, *Ptolemaic Alexandria,* 3 vols. (Oxford: Oxford University Press, 1972), esp. vol. 1, chap. 2, and Victor Tcherikover, *Hellenistic Civilization and the Jews,* trans. S. Applebaum (New York: Atheneum, 1979), esp. pt. 2, chap. 2.

4. See Benjamin Braude and Bernard Lewis, eds. *Christians and Jews in the Ottoman Empire: The Functioning of a Plural Society,* vol. 1: *The Central Lands* (New York: Holmes and Meier, 1982) for the historical story, and Will Kymlicka, "Two Models of Pluralism and Tolerance," in *Toleration: An Elusive Virtue,* pp. 81–105, for a theoretical account of the millet system as

"a useful reminder that individual rights are not the only way to accommodate religious pluralism."

5. On the location of these limits, see my debate with David Luban in Charles Beitz, Marshall Cohen, Thomas Scanlon, and A. John Simmons, eds. *International Ethics* (Princeton, N.J.: Princeton University Press, 1985), pp. 165-243.

6. These examples of intolerance short of armed intervention were suggested to me by John Rawls.

7. See Arend Lijphart, *Democracy in Plural Societies: A Comparative Exploration* (New Haven: Yale University Press, 1977).

8. On German Jews, a prototypical minority, see H. I. Bach, *The German Jew: A Synthesis of Judaism and Western Civilization, 1730-1930* (Oxford: Oxford University Press, 1984) and Donald L. Niewyk, *The Jews in Weimar Germany* (Baton Rouge: Louisiana State University Press, 1980).

9. This is the argument of Will Kymlicka in his *Multicultural Citizenship* (New York: Oxford University Press, 1995), who applies it specifically to conquered minorities, like the aboriginal societies of the new world. It applies in principle to any long-standing, territorially based minority group, but not to groups of immigrants—for reasons I explain, following Kymlicka, in the next section.

10. Both this and the previous quotation are taken from Patrick Thornberry, *International Law and the Rights of Minorities* (Oxford: Oxford University Press, 1991); see his discussion of the treaties, pp. 132-37.

11. I rely on the United States as my key example here, and John Higham as my chief guide to the politics of American immigration: see *Strangers in the Land* and also *Send These to Me: Jews and Other Immigrants in Urban America* (New York: Atheneum, 1975). I have also drawn on the articles and essays in Stephan Thernstrom, ed., *Harvard Encyclopedia of American Ethnic Groups* (Cambridge, Mass.: Harvard University Press, 1980)—and on my own account of American pluralism, *What It Means to Be an American* (New York: Marsilio, 1992) as well as, of course, my own experience of that pluralism.

12. I owe these examples to Clifford Geertz.

CHAPTER 3: COMPLICATED CASES

1. See William Rogers Brubaker, ed. *Immigration and the Politics of Citizenship in Europe and North America* (Lanham, Md.: University Press of America [for the German Marshall Fund], 1989), p. 7.

2. The actual story is more complicated than this brief summary suggests. Rogers Brubaker, in his *Citizenship and Nationhood in France and Germany* (Cambridge, Mass.: Harvard University Press, 1992) provides an excellent account.

3. For an analysis of the debate, see Gary Kates, "Jews into French-

men: Nationality and Representation in Revolutionary France," *Social Research* 56 (spring 1989): 229.

4. Jean-Paul Sartre, *Anti-Semite and Jew,* trans. George J. Becker, preface by Michael Walzer (New York: Schocken, 1995), pp. 56–57.

5. But the word *francisation* does figure in the current debates in Quebec.

6. For a useful account of some of these tensions, see Dan Horowitz and Moshe Lissak, *Trouble in Utopia: The Overburdened Polity of Israel* (Albany: State University of New York Press, 1989).

7. Alex Weingrod, "Palestinian Israelis?" in *Dissent* (summer 1996): 108–10.

8. James Tully, *Strange Multiplicity: Constitutionalism in an Age of Diversity* (Cambridge: Cambridge University Press, 1995), pp. 145–46. Tully provides an excellent account of the dilemmas of toleration in Canada as well as a strong defense of Québecois, and especially Aboriginal, rights. For a useful liberal corrective closer to my own view here, see Kymlicka, *Multicultural Citizenship.*

9. See Charles Taylor's collected essays on Canadian ethnic politics: *Reconciling the Solitudes: Essays on Canadian Federalism and Nationalism,* ed. Guy Laforest (Montreal: McGill-Queens University Press, 1993).

10. Martin Holland, *European Integration: From Community to Union* (London: Pinter Publishers, 1994), p. 156. See also the discussion of "new social rights in Europe" in Maurice Roche, *Rethinking Citizenship: Welfare, Ideology and Change in Modern Society* (Cambridge: Polity Press, 1992), chap. 8.

CHAPTER 4: PRACTICAL ISSUES

1. Cf. Stephen L. Carter, *The Culture of Disbelief* (New York: Basic Books, 1993), p. 96: "the language of tolerance is the language of power."

2. See Ralph Ellison's classic novel, *Invisible Man* (New York: Random House, 1952).

3. Readers may find it useful to look at a case study outside my range of comparison: Marc Galanter's *Competing Equalities: Law and the Backward Classes in India* (Berkeley: University of California Press, 1984). The Indian version of "compensatory discrimination" was specifically designed to overcome an age-old regime of stigmatization and intolerance, and Galanter argues that the effort to do that by producing a class of civil servants among the "untouchables" has brought India at least some way, but only some way, toward that goal.

4. Sir Percival Griffiths, *The British Impact on India* (London: Mac-Donald, 1952), pp. 222, 224.

5. I am following the account of Bronwyn Winter, "Women, the Law, and Cultural Relativism in France: The Case of Excision," *Signs* 19 (summer 1994), pp. 939–74.

6. Quoted in ibid., p. 951, from a petition drafted by Martine Lefeuvre and published in 1989 by the Mouvement Anti-Utilitariste dans les Sciences Sociales (MAUSS). I have revised the translation.

7. Ibid., p. 957.

8. I should stress that my argument isn't meant to require the criminalization of these practices, only some form of state intervention aimed at stopping them. Winter makes a strong case for efforts to reshape the processes of cultural reproduction: adult education, medical counseling, and so on (ibid., pp. 966–72). For another case study whose author reaches similar conclusions, see Raphael Cohen-Almagor, "Female Circumcision and Murder for Family Honour Among Minorities in Israel," in Kirsten E. Schulze, Martin Stokes, and Colm Campbell, *Nationalism, Minorities and Diasporas: Identities and Rights in the Middle East* (London: I. B. Tauris, 1996), pp. 171–87.

9. See the innovative argument of Anna Elisabetta Galleoti in her "Citizenship and Equality: The Place for Toleration," *Political Theory* 21 (Nov. 1993): 585–605. I have benefited from conversations with Dr. Galleoti about the problems of toleration in contemporary Europe.

10. For a strong argument (which seems to me too strong) against this compromise arrangement, see Ian Shapiro, *Democracy's Place* (Ithaca, N.Y.: Cornell University Press, 1996), chap. 6: "Democratic Autonomy and Religious Freedom: A Critique of *Wisconsin v. Yoder*" (written with Richard Arneson) and Amy Gutmann, "Civil Education and Social Diversity," *Ethics* 105 (Apr. 1995): 557–79.

11. See the collection of legal texts, speeches, and tracts in Lillian Schlissel, ed., *Conscience in America* (New York: E. P. Dutton, 1968).

12. For a strong and substantive account of the educational requirements of liberal democracy, see Amy Gutmann, *Democratic Education* (Princeton, N.J.: Princeton University Press, 1987).

13. *The Social Contract,* bk. 4, chap. 8; the application of this term to contemporary civil religious practices is the work of Robert Bellah: see *The Broken Covenant: American Civil Religion in Time of Trial* (New York: Seabury, 1975).

14. For a different view of fundamentalist objections to liberal education, see Nomi Maya Stolzenberg, " 'He Drew a Circle That Shut Me Out': Assimilation, Indoctrination, and the Paradox of Liberal Education," *Harvard Law Review* 106 (1993): 581–667. The paradox is real enough, and yet the parents about whom Stolzenberg writes so sympathetically, fundamentalist Christians, probably exaggerate the effect of the public schools on their children. Nonetheless, conscientious objection by such parents and their children might be permitted in a liberal society: see Sanford Levinson's review of Stephen Carter's *Culture of Disbelief* in the *Michigan Law Review* 92, no. 6 (May 1994): 1873–92.

15. The establishment of Labor Day as a public holiday in the United States provides an interesting example of what can and can't (or should

and shouldn't) be done. May Day was the holiday of the labor movement and of the various parties and sects allied with it; it had a specific and restrictive political meaning that probably made it unsuitable for national observance. The holiday's new name and date opened the way for a nonspecific and nonideological celebration not so much of the movement of working men and women as of the men and women themselves.

16. Cf. Herbert Marcuse's argument for much more radical limits: "the withdrawal of tolerance before the deed, at the stage of communication in word, print, and picture" ("Repressive Tolerance," in Robert Paul Wolff, Barrington Moore, Jr., and Herbert Marcuse, *A Critique of Pure Tolerance* [Boston: Beacon, 1965], p. 109). Marcuse's argument follows from an extraordinary confidence in his own ability to recognize "the forces of emancipation" and so to refuse toleration only to their enemies.

CHAPTER 5: MODERN AND POSTMODERN TOLERATION

1. Jean-Paul Sartre's well-known argument that anti-Semitism is what sustains Jewish identity can be repeated for many other minority groups, but it is unlikely to be accepted by their members (especially their most committed members), who attach real value to the group's history and culture and assume that this value is what generates individual identification. See my preface to *Anti-Semite and Jew.*

2. This line is spoken by a character in Robert Frost's narrative poem "Mending Wall" (*The Poems of Robert Frost* [New York: Modern Library, 1946], pp. 35-36). The poet does not wholly endorse it.

3. Julia Kristeva, *Nations Without Nationalism,* trans. Leon S. Roudiez (New York: Columbia University Press, 1993), p. 21 and passim. See also Kristeva, *Strangers to Ourselves,* trans. Leon S. Roudiez (New York: Columbia University Press, 1991).

4. Kristeva, *Nations Without Nationalism,* pp. 35-43.

EPILOGUE: REFLECTIONS ON AMERICAN MULTICULTURALISM

1. (New York: Knopf, 1963).

2. Irving Howe makes the same point with regard to left-wing political associations in his book *Socialism and America* (San Diego: Harcourt Brace Jovanovich, 1985), where he describes how socialist militants became union organizers and officials and then moved into positions in local and state Democratic Party campaigns. This view of socialism as a "prep school" for mainstream parties and movements is, Howe argues, no comfort for socialists. Entering the mainstream is often, in fact, a painful business. See his account, pp. 78-81, 141.

3. This is the argument of Robert Putnam in a number of papers

that are not yet (at this writing) in book form. I have heard critics argue that there are in fact associations that are growing in the United States today—staff organizations of various sorts that provide services to their members (like the American Association of Retired Persons), therapeutic groups (like Alcoholics Anonymous), networks in cyberspace, and so on. But it isn't clear that these groups provide the same education in and discipline for common work that was provided by the parties, movements, and churches with which Putnam is primarily concerned. See his "Bowling Alone: America's Declining Social Capital," *Journal of Democracy* 6 (Jan. 1995): 65–78.

4. Most of the information in the following list comes from U.S. Bureau of the Census, *Statistical Abstract of the United States: 1994,* 114th ed. (Washington D.C., 1994); see also Andrew Hacker's useful *U/S: A Statistical Portrait of the American People* (New York: Viking, 1983).

5. This is an exaggeration of the argument of Arthur M. Schlesinger, Jr.'s *The Disuniting of America* (New York: Norton, 1992), but not of what followed its publication—on radio and television, in newspaper editorials and columns, in the magazines, and so on.

6. A. D. Lindsay, *The Modern Democratic State,* vol. 1 (there was no second volume) (London: Oxford University Press, 1943), chap. 5.

7. See John Kenneth Galbraith, *American Capitalism: The Concept of Countervailing Power* (Boston: Houghton Mifflin, 1952), and Richard B. Freeman and James L. Medoff, *What Do Unions Do?* (New York: Basic Books, 1984).

8. Gabriel A. Almond and Sidney Verba, *The Civic Culture: Political Attitudes and Democracy in Five Nations* (Princeton, N.J.: Princeton University Press, 1963), esp. chap. 10.

9. See the argument in Gutmann, *Democratic Education.*

Acknowledgments

This book has a complicated history. It started as a lecture, sponsored by the Unione Italiana del Lavoro, sketching the five "regimes of toleration," delivered in Palermo and again in Florence and then again at a conference on nationalism organized by Robert McKim and Jeff McMahan at the University of Illinois (a conference volume will be published by Oxford University Press). I traveled for a while giving the lecture and received useful comments and some sharp criticism from friends and colleagues in Italy, Canada, England, Germany, Austria, the Netherlands, and the United States. Although I can't list here the many people who helped me think about the problems of toleration along the way, I am grateful to all of them. A few of them are more specifically acknowledged in the endnotes.

I began expanding the lecture to deal with their comments and then wrote a parallel piece, published in *Dissent* (spring 1994) under the title "Multiculturalism and Individualism," on how toleration "works" in the United States. Discussions with colleagues and visitors at the Institute for Advanced Study in Princeton led me to revise both the lecture and the article. The committee for the Castle Lectures gave me a splendid opportunity to bring the pieces together and to test their coherence in front of a lively and engaged audience at Yale. Ian Shapiro organized my visit to New Haven and helped me decide to think about this book *as* a book. Readers for Yale University Press provided a final set of comments and criticism; three readers, Jane Mansbridge, Susan Okin, and Bernard Yack, shed their anonymity and so made it possible for me to thank them here. I followed many of their suggestions. This book would no doubt be better (but also longer) had I attended to all of them.

Index